Daily Fundamentals

GRADE 1

Editorial Development: Teera Safi
Lisa Vitarisi Mathews
Copy Editing: Laurie Westrich
Art Direction: Yuki Meyer
Design/Production: Jessica Onken
Susan Lovell

EMC 3241

Evan-Moor
Helping Children Learn

Visit
teaching-standards.com
to view a correlation
of this book.
This is a free service.

**Correlated to
Current Standards**

**Congratulations on your purchase of some of the
finest teaching materials in the world.**

*Photocopying the pages in this book
is permitted for <u>single-classroom use only</u>.
Making photocopies for additional classes
or schools is prohibited.*

CPSIA: McNaughton & Gunn, Saline, MI USA [12/2020]

CONTENTS

What's Inside?

Daily Fundamentals has 30 weeks of cross-curricular skills practice. Each week provides targeted practice with language, math, and reading skills. The focused daily tasks progress in difficulty as students move from Day 1 tasks to Day 5 tasks. Item types range from multiple choice and matching to constructed response and open-ended questions.

Language items practice grammar, mechanics, spelling, and vocabulary.

Math items practice number and operations, algebraic thinking, geometry, measurement and data, and problem solving.

Reading items practice core reading comprehension skills such as inference, prediction, author's purpose, main idea and details, summary, fact and opinion, nonfiction text features, and literary analysis.

One language skill is practiced each week. A variety of item types provides rigorous practice and adds interest.

Math items focus on one concept or skill each week and provide opportunities for applying a variety of strategies.

Reading items target one reading comprehension or analysis skill each week and are based on nonfiction and fiction text selections. Questions elicit the use of multiple levels of thinking skills.

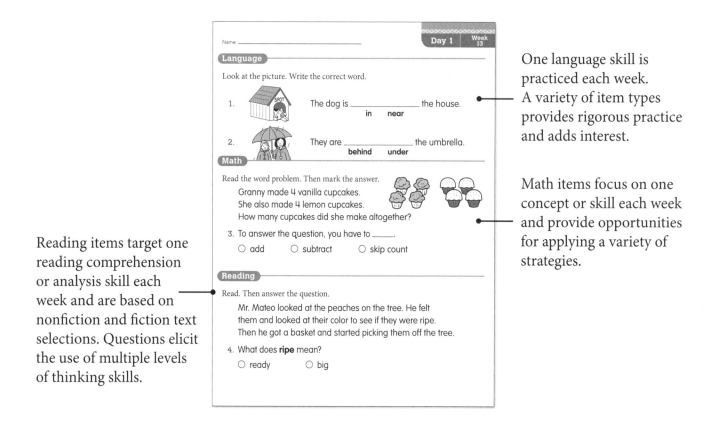

Answer Key

Correct or exemplar responses are shown on a reduced version of the actual page. An * is used to indicate an open-ended item or an item with many ways to word the answer. Accept any reasonable response.

How to Use This Book

Using *Daily Fundamentals* with Students Who Are Reading

Have the daily practice activity on students' desks when they arrive in the morning, after recess, or during a transitional period. Have students complete the assignment independently. Then have them share their answers and the strategy or approach they used. Encourage discussion about each item so students can share their thinking and provide support and insights to one another. These discussions may also provide you with teachable moments and information to guide your instruction.

Using *Daily Fundamentals* with Emergent Readers

Distribute the daily activity to each student. Ask students to point to the first item as you read aloud the directions. Demonstrate or explain how to complete the first item. Have students complete the next item independently. Repeat the process for the math and reading items. After students complete all of the items, review the answers as a whole group. Invite students to share their answers and talk about their thinking. As an alternative, you may wish to have students complete the activity in pairs, pairing more advanced students with students who need support.

Using *Daily Fundamentals* as an Informal Assessment

You may wish to use the weekly lessons as an informal assessment of students' competencies. Because each week's practice focuses on a particular skill or concept, the tasks provide you with a detailed view of each student's level of mastery.

Skills Scope and Sequence

Use the scope and sequence chart to identify the specific skills that students are practicing.

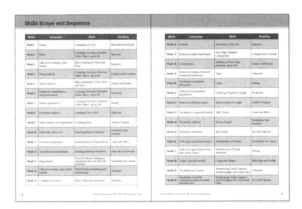

Student Progress Chart

Students can monitor their own progress by recording their daily scores and thinking about their success with different skills. Reproduce and distribute the progress chart to students at the beginning of each week. For older students, you may wish to have them write the number correct out of the total number of items.

Student Record Sheet

Record students' scores on the record sheet. This form will provide you with a snapshot of each student's skills mastery in language, math, and reading and serve as a resource to track students' progress throughout the year.

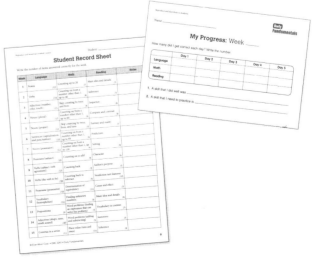

Skills Scope and Sequence

Week	Language	Math	Reading
Week 1	Nouns	Counting Up to 20	Main Idea and Details
Week 2	Verbs	Counting On from a Number Other Than 1, up to 40	Inference
Week 3	Adjectives (number, color, touch)	Skip Counting by Twos and Fives	Sequence
Week 4	Nouns (plural)	Counting On from a Number Other Than 1, up to 60	Compare and Contrast
Week 5	Nouns (proper)	Skip Counting by Twos, Fives, and Tens	Fantasy and Reality
Week 6	Sentences (capitalization, end punctuation)	Counting On from a Number Other Than 1, up to 85	Prediction
Week 7	Nouns (possessive)	Counting On from a Number Other Than 1, up to 120	Setting
Week 8	Pronouns (subject)	Counting On to Add	Character
Week 9	Verbs (subject-verb agreement)	Counting Back	Author's Purpose
Week 10	Verbs (the verb *to be*)	Counting Back to Subtract	Nonfiction Text Features
Week 11	Pronouns (possessive)	Determination of Equivalency	Cause and Effect
Week 12	Vocabulary (homophones)	Finding Unknown Numbers	Main Idea and Details
Week 13	Prepositions	Word Problems (finding an expression that can solve the problem)	Vocabulary in Context
Week 14	Adjectives (shape, taste, smell, sound)	Word Problems (adding and subtracting)	Summary
Week 15	Commas in a Series	Place Value (tens and ones)	Inference

Daily Fundamentals • EMC 3241 • © Evan-Moor Corp.

Week	Language	Math	Reading
Week 16	Adverbs	Ten More or Ten Less	Sequence
Week 17	Sentences (subject/predicate)	Two-Digit Numbers Comparison	Compare and Contrast
Week 18	Contractions	Addition of Two-Digit Numbers, up to 100	Fantasy and Reality
Week 19	Sentences (conjunctions and compound sentences)	Time	Character
Week 20	Vocabulary (synonyms, antonyms)	Coins	Setting
Week 21	Adjectives (comparative, superlative)	Ordering Objects by Length	Prediction
Week 22	Sentences (different types)	Measurement of Length	Author's Purpose
Week 23	Vocabulary (compound words)	Tally Charts	Cause and Effect
Week 24	Vocabulary (affixes)	Picture Graphs	Nonfiction Text Features
Week 25	Pronouns (indefinite)	Bar Graphs	Fact and Opinion
Week 26	Verbs (past and future tenses)	Identification of Shapes	Vocabulary in Context
Week 27	Adjectives (good, better, best; bad, worse, worst)	Identification of Shape Attributes	Setting
Week 28	Usage (confused words)	Composite Shapes	Main Idea and Details
Week 29	Vocabulary in Context	Partitioning Circles, Squares, and Rectangles into Equal Parts	Character
Week 30	Vocabulary (real-life connections between words and their use)	Partitioning Circles, Squares, and Rectangles into Fractional Parts	Fact and Opinion

Name _____

My Progress: Week _____

How many did I get correct each day? Write the number.

	Day 1	Day 2	Day 3	Day 4	Day 5
Language					
Math					
Reading					

1. A skill that I did well was _____.

2. A skill that I need to practice is _____.

--✂------

Daily
Fundamentals

Name _____

My Progress: Week _____

How many did I get correct each day? Write the number.

	Day 1	Day 2	Day 3	Day 4	Day 5
Language					
Math					
Reading					

1. A skill that I did well was _____.

2. A skill that I need to practice is _____.

Reproduce and record each student's scores.

Student: ______________________

Student Record Sheet

Write the number of items answered correctly for the week.

Week	Language	Math	Reading	Notes
1	Nouns /15	Counting up to 20 /7	Main idea and details /5	
2	Verbs /14	Counting on from a number other than 1, up to 40 /6	Inference /5	
3	Adjectives (number, color, touch) /15	Skip counting by twos and fives /6	Sequence /8	
4	Nouns (plural) /15	Counting on from a number other than 1, up to 60 /6	Compare and contrast /8	
5	Nouns (proper) /11	Skip counting by twos, fives, and tens /5	Fantasy and reality /7	
6	Sentences (capitalization, end punctuation) /10	Counting on from a number other than 1, up to 85 /6	Prediction /6	
7	Nouns (possessive) /12	Counting on from a number other than 1, up to 120 /6	Setting /8	
8	Pronouns (subject) /10	Counting on to add /6	Character /6	
9	Verbs (subject-verb agreement) /15	Counting back /5	Author's purpose /5	
10	Verbs (the verb *to be*) /20	Counting back to subtract /6	Nonfiction text features /10	
11	Pronouns (possessive) /10	Determination of equivalency /14	Cause and effect /5	
12	Vocabulary (homophones) /14	Finding unknown numbers /6	Main idea and details /6	
13	Prepositions /9	Word problems (finding an expression that can solve the problem) /5	Vocabulary in context /5	
14	Adjectives (shape, taste, smell, sound) /20	Word problems (adding and subtracting) /5	Summary /5	
15	Commas in a series /11	Place value (tens and ones) /14	Inference /8	

Student Record Sheet, *continued*

Week	Language	Math	Reading	Notes
16	Adverbs /15	Ten more or ten less /12	Sequence /9	
17	Sentences (subject/predicate) /15	Two-digit numbers comparison /17	Compare and contrast /7	
18	Contractions /12	Addition of two-digit numbers, up to 100 /13	Fantasy and reality /8	
19	Sentences (conjunctions and compound sentences) /7	Time /15	Character /5	
20	Vocabulary (synonyms, antonyms) /19	Coins /12	Setting /10	
21	Adjectives (comparative, superlative) /14	Ordering objects by length /14	Prediction /5	
22	Sentences (different types) /16	Measurement of length /9	Author's purpose /6	
23	Vocabulary (compound words) /19	Tally charts /10	Cause and effect /5	
24	Vocabulary (affixes) /11	Picture graphs /5	Nonfiction text features /9	
25	Pronouns (indefinite) /10	Bar graphs /7	Fact and opinion /6	
26	Verbs (past and future tenses) /14	Identification of shapes /13	Vocabulary in context /9	
27	Adjectives (good, better, best; bad, worse, worst) /13	Identification of shape attributes /16	Setting /8	
28	Usage (confused words) /15	Composite shapes /12	Main idea and details /7	
29	Vocabulary in context /5	Partitioning circles, squares, and rectangles into equal parts /21	Character /7	
30	Vocabulary (real-life connections between words and their use) /5	Partitioning circles, squares, and rectangles into fractional parts /14	Fact and opinion /9	

Daily Fundamentals • EMC 3241 • © Evan-Moor Corp.

Language

Mark the circle that names a **person**.

1. ○ sit   ○ boy

2. ○ mom   ○ see

3. ○ run   ○ man

Math

Count how many. Write the number.

4.

_____ frogs

5.

_____ butterflies

Reading

Read. Then answer the question.

Pat has a cat. Pat has a rat.
Her cat is on a mat. Her rat has a hat.

6. Who is this story about?

○ Pat and her pets

○ a mat and a hat

Language

Mark the circle that names a **place**.

1. ○ park   ○ play

2. ○ help   ○ school

3. ○ get   ○ home

Math

Count how many in each group. Circle the group that has 8.

4.

Reading

Read. Then answer the question.

What did I do today?
I had fun.
I ate a hot dog on a bun.
I sat in the sun.

5. What is this story about?

○ a sunny day

○ a boy who had fun

Language

Mark the circle that names a **thing**.

1. ○ like   ○ book

2. ○ hat   ○ cook

3. ○ sat   ○ fan

Math

Count how many. Write the number.

4.

_____ dots

5.

_____ dots

Reading

Read. Then answer the question.

Mom can mop. I can hop.
Tim can pop. Dad can chop.
We can not stop.
We can mop, hop, pop, and chop!

6. What is this story about?

○ where people can go

○ what people can do

Language

Mark the circle that names an **animal**.

1. ○ pig   ○ wig

2. ○ mat   ○ cat

3. ○ bug   ○ rug

Math

Count to 15. Then draw 15 dots in the box.

4.

Reading

Read. Then answer the question.

I see a bug on a rug. Come here, bug!
Now the bug is on the mug. Come here, bug!
Now the bug is on me.
I will give the bug a hug.

5. What is this story about?

○ a boy and a bug

○ a rug and a mug

Language

A noun is a person, place, animal, or thing. Circle the noun.

1. The girl hops.

2. The man sits.

3. This is the park.

Math

Count to 20. Write the numbers on the lines.

4. ____ ____ ____ ____ ____ ____ ____

____ ____ ____ ____ ____ ____ ____

____ ____ ____ ____ ____ _20_

Reading

Read. Then answer the question.

My name is Jill. I am going to a farm.
I want to see where sheep live.
I want to see sheep eat.
I want to pet sheep.

5. What is this story about?

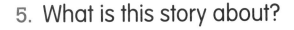

_____

Language

Circle the word that tells what the boy is doing.

1. The boy jumps.

2. The boy eats.

3. The boy sleeps.

Math

Read the problem. Count on to answer the question.

4. There are 17 eggs in the basket. How many eggs are there in all?

_____ eggs in all

Reading

Read. Then answer the question.

Mom says I need to wash.
I do not like the tub!
I do not like to scrub.
Today Mom gave me a toy sub.
I want to get in the tub.
I want to scrub.
I will have fun in the tub.

5. Why does the boy like the tub now?

○ because he has a toy

○ because he likes to wash

Language

What do the kids **do**? Mark the circle.

1. The kids walk home.

   ○ home   ○ walk

2. The kids eat food.

   ○ eat   ○ food

3. The kids play ball.

   ○ play   ○ ball

Math

Count on. Write all the numbers. Then write how many in all.

4.

18

_____   _____   _____

_____ hearts in all

Reading

Read. Then answer the question.

What is in the pot?
It is not cold. It is hot.
It smells good.
It will hit the spot!

5. What do you think is in the pot?

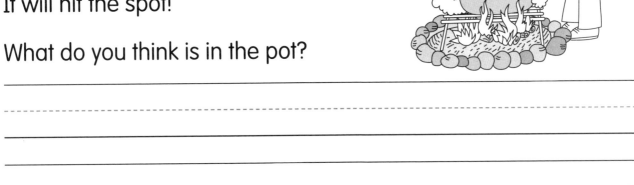

_____

_____

_____

Language

What do the people **do**? Mark the circle.

1. Dad makes cake.
   ○ makes   ○ cake

2. Mom cooks ham.
   ○ ham   ○ cooks

3. Liz plays ball.
   ○ plays   ○ ball

Math

Count on. Write how many.

4.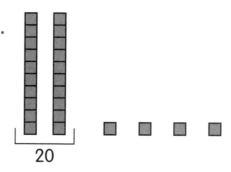

   20

   _____ cubes

Reading

Read. Answer the question. Then draw.

Kit bit and bit. She will not quit!
Paper here. Paper there.
What a mess!
Sit, Kit, sit! Good girl!

5. Who or what do you think Kit is?
   ○ a girl
   ○ a dog
   ○ a toy

Draw a picture of Kit.

Language

Circle the action word.

1. Tran reads his book.

2. Kim pets the dog.

3. Jeff rides his bike.

Math

Use the number line to count on.
Write the numbers.

4.
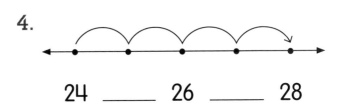

24 _____ 26 _____ 28

5.
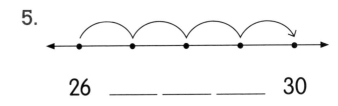

26 _____ _____ _____ 30

Reading

Read the story. Then answer the question.

Goodbye summer.
I know it is fall.
The wind is here.
The wind is here every day.

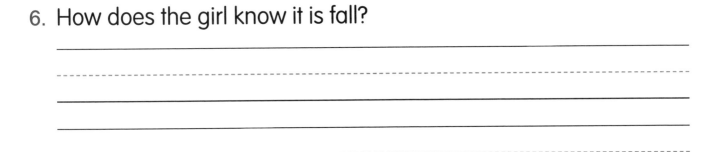

6. How does the girl know it is fall?

_____

- -

_____

- -

_____

Language

Finish the sentence. Write an action word.

hops   sits

1. The bunny _____ .

2. The man _____ .

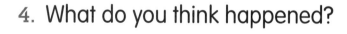

Math

Count on to finish the chart. Write the numbers.

3.

25		27	
29		31	
33			36
37			40

Reading

Read. Then answer the question.

There was a bird that had a nest.
The nest was in an apple tree.
A cat looked at the bird.
Then up and up went the cat.
Then down and down went the cat.
Where was that bird?

4. What do you think happened?

_____
_____
_____

Name _____

Language

Circle the word that tells about **size**.

1. My dad is tall.

2. My sister is small.

3. My pet is big.

Math

Skip count by twos. Write the numbers.

4.

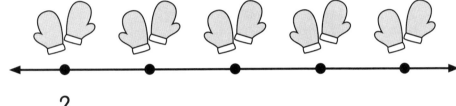

2 _____ _____ _____ _____

Reading

Read. Then answer the items.

What I Do

① I wake up.

② I get dressed.

③ I eat.

④ I brush my teeth.

⑤ I go to school.

5. Is this list in the right order?

○ yes   ○ no

6. Tell why or why not.

_____

_____

Language

Circle the word that tells **how many**.

1. I see two bikes.

2. I want one bike.

3. I will ride it five times.

Math

Skip count by twos. Write the numbers.

4.

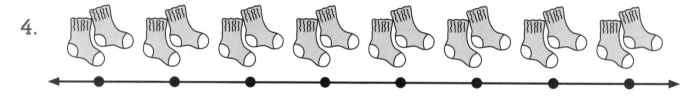

____   ____   ____   ____   ____   ____   ____   ____

Reading

Read. Then answer the question.

How does a bird make a nest? First, it finds a tree. Next, it finds twigs and straw. Last, it makes the nest. Now it has a home!

5. What is the second thing a bird does to make a nest?

_____

_____

Language

Circle the word that tells about **color**.

1. I have pink toes.

2. My sister has blue eyes.

3. My brother has brown hair.

Math

Skip count by fives. Write the numbers.

4.

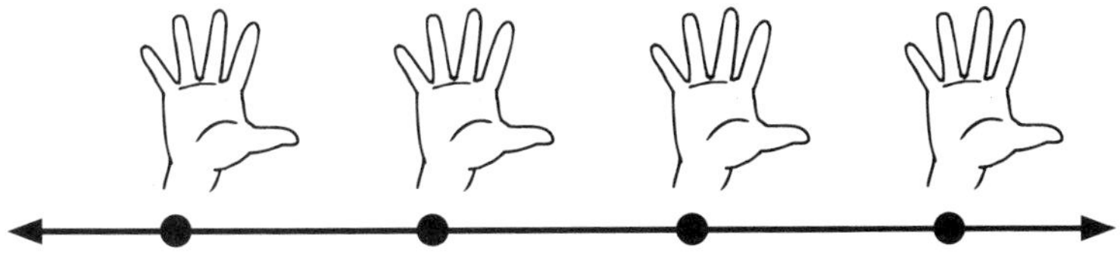

5 ____ ____ ____

Reading

Read. Then answer the questions.

Today was a big day for Jen. First, she made her bed. Then, she put away her toys. Next, she made a card. Last, she said, "Happy birthday, Mom!"

5. What did Jen do first?

○ put away her toys

○ made her bed

6. What did Jen do third?

_____

_____

Language

Which word tells how something **feels**?

1. The water is warm. ○ water ○ warm

2. The grass feels wet. ○ wet ○ the

3. The cat's fur is soft. ○ cat's ○ soft

Math

Skip count by fives. Write the numbers.

4.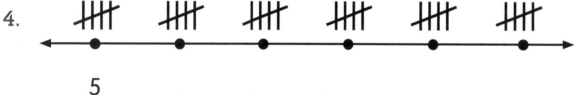

   5 ____ ____ ____ ____ ____

Reading

Read. Then write 1, 2, 3, 4 to tell what happened.

Dad fills a tub with water. Spot jumps in the tub. Dad scrubs Spot. Spot jumps out of the tub.

5. _____ Dad scrubs Spot.   _____ Spot jumps in the tub.

   _____ Spot jumps out of   _____ Dad fills a tub with
         the tub.   water.

Language

Write the word that tells about the dog.

1. It is a small dog. _____

2. The dog is brown. _____

3. The dog is furry. _____

Math

Look at the numbers. Then answer the items.

2, 4, 6, 8, 10, 12, 14, 16, 18, 20, 22, 24, 26, 28, 30

4. Is this skip counting?   ○ yes   ○ no

5. This skip counting is by _____.   ○ twos   ○ fives

Reading

Read. Then answer the items.

1. Put on your shoes.

2. Put on your socks.

3. Tie your shoes.

6. Is this list in the right order?   7. Tell why or why not.

○ yes   ○ no

_____

_____

Language

Circle the word that names **more than one**.

1. girls   girl

2. balls   ball

3. hat   hats

Math

Read the problem. Count on to answer the question.

4. There are 28 cookies in the jar. How many cookies are there in all?

28

_____ cookies in all

Reading

Read. Then answer the question.

I have two pets. I have a cat and a dog. My dog plays all day. My cat sleeps all day. My cat and dog eat at night.

5. How are the cat and the dog the same?

○ They eat at night.

○ They play all day.

Language

Circle the word that names **more than one**.

1. hand   hands

2. apples   apple

3. cow   cows

Math

Count on. Write all the numbers. Then write how many in all.

4.

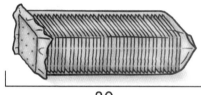

30

_____   _____   _____

_____   _____   _____

_____ crackers in all

Reading

Read. Then answer the question.

Kim and Tom both have bikes. Kim's bike is blue. Tom's bike is green. Both of the bikes have white tires.

5. How are the bikes the same?

_____

Language

Write **s** to make a word that names **more than one**.

1. The boy_____ play.

2. The owl_____ hoot.

3. The bat_____ fly.

Math

Count on. Write how many.

4.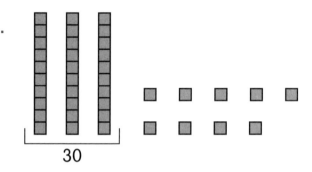

30

_____ cubes

Reading

Read. Then answer the questions.

Marti has a brother and a sister.
Her brother is small. Her sister is big.
Both her brother and sister have red hair.

5. How are Marti's brother and sister different?

_____

6. How are Marti's brother and sister the same?

_____

Language

Write **es** to make a word that names **more than one**.

1. I see the box_____.

2. I like dress_____.

3. I make wish_____.

Math

Use the number line to count on.

4.

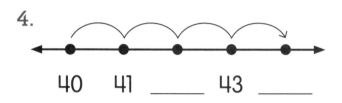

40   41   ____   43   ____

5.

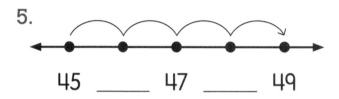

45   ____   47   ____   49

Reading

Read. Then answer the items.

> Kevin likes to read books. His friend Rick likes to color. Kevin and Rick both like to play outside.

6. Kevin and Rick are the same because _____.

   ○ they both like to read

   ○ they both like to play outside

7. Kevin and Rick are different because _____.

   ○ Kevin likes to read, and Rick likes to color

   ○ Kevin likes to play outside, and Rick likes to color

Language

Circle the word that goes with the picture.

1.  box   boxes

2.  rats   rat

3.  bird   birds

Math

Count on to finish the chart. Write the numbers.

4.

45			48
	50	51	
53	54		56
	58		60

Reading

Read. Then answer the questions.

Many animals live in ponds.
Frogs live in ponds. Frogs hop to the pond.
Ducks live in ponds. Ducks fly to the pond.
Both frogs and ducks like water.

5. What is the same about frogs and ducks?

_____

6. What is different about frogs and ducks?

_____

Daily Fundamentals • EMC 3241 • © Evan-Moor Corp.

Language

Does it need a capital letter? Write the word or words to finish the sentence.

1. _____ is my friend.

   Susan   **susan**

2. I saw _____ at school.

   Mr. Lee   **mr. lee**

Math

Skip count by fives. Write the numbers.

3.

5   ____   ____   ____   ____   ____   ____   ____

Reading

Read. Then answer the question.

"Hello, Horse, do you know it is my birthday?" said Cow. Horse said, "Oh, I know it is your birthday. I made a cake for you. It is a cake made of very good grass." "Thank you, Horse!" said Cow.

4. Is this story real or make-believe?

_____

Language

Does it need a capital letter? Write the word to finish the sentence.

1. Mary lives in _____.

   texas   **Texas**

2. She goes to _____ School.

   manza   **Manza**

Math

Skip count by fives. Write the numbers.

3. 5, _____, _____, 20, _____, _____,

   35, _____, 45, _____

Reading

Read. Then answer the question.

The sun gives us light.
The sun keeps us warm.
People need the sun to live.
Plants need the sun to live.
Animals need the sun to live.

4. Is this story real or make-believe?

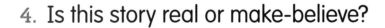

Language

Does it need a capital letter? Write the word to finish the sentence.

1. Mom's birthday is on _____.

   Monday   monday

2. I was born in _____, too.

   april   April

Math

Skip count by tens. Write the numbers.

3.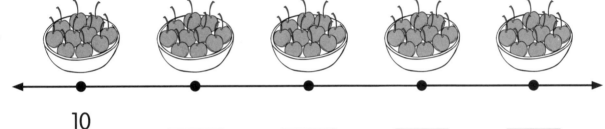

10 _____ _____ _____ _____

Reading

Read. Then answer the items.

Wind is all around. It blows all over the world.
We cannot see the wind, but we can see what it does.
Wind can move the leaves on a tree.

4. This is about something _____.

   ○ real   ○ make-believe

5. Tell how you know.

Language

Does it need a capital letter? Write the underlined word or words correctly.

1. Miss <u>banks</u> is nice.   _____

2. My dog <u>spike</u> is big.   _____

3. I live on <u>first street</u>.   _____

Math

Skip count by fives. Write the numbers.

4. 5, _____, _____, _____, _____, _____,

_____, _____, _____, _____, _____

Reading

Read. Then answer the items.

Ricky Rabbit loves apples. He told his brother to climb the apple tree and throw down some apples. "Ouch, ouch!" said Ricky Rabbit. "Is that enough?" yelled his brother.

5. This is about something _____.

   ○ real   ○ make-believe

6. Tell how you know.

_____

Language

Does it need a capital letter? Write the word(s) correctly to finish the sentence.

> mr. roger   thanksgiving

1. Have you seen _____?

2. We eat pie on _____.

Math

Skip count by tens. Write the numbers.

3. 10, _____, _____, 40, _____,

   60, _____, 80, _____, 100

Reading

Read. Then answer the question.

> This bird is a robin. People like to watch robins eat. Robins run to look for food. When they see a worm, they pull it out of the ground.

4. Is this about something real or make-believe? Tell how you know.

_____

_____

Language

What does a sentence need? Mark **yes** or **no** to tell if it is a sentence.

1. john is seven

   ○ yes   ○ no

2. John is seven.

   ○ yes   ○ no

Math

Read the problem. Count on to answer the question.

3. There are 48 bees in the hive. How many bees are there in all?

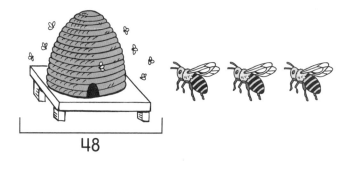

48

_____ bees in all

Reading

Read. Then answer the items.

The sky looked gray.
It felt cold outside.
All of a sudden, I felt
one wet drop on my hand.

4. What do you think will happen next?

_____

5. Tell why.

_____

Language

What does a sentence need? Mark **yes** or **no** to tell if it is a sentence.

1. I will play soccer.

   ○ yes   ○ no

2. i will play soccer

   ○ yes   ○ no

Math

Count on. Write all the numbers. Then write how many in all.

3.

50

_____ pieces of popcorn in all

Reading

Read. Then answer the question.

Mama Chick sat on her four eggs every day. On Thursday, she felt something move. She got off her nest and saw two chicks break out of their eggs. On Friday, Mama Chick heard something.

4. What do you think Mama Chick will do next?

_____

_____

Language

Mark **yes** or **no** to tell if it is a sentence.

1. How are you?

   ○ yes   ○ no

2. how are you

   ○ yes   ○ no

Math

Count on. Write how many.

3.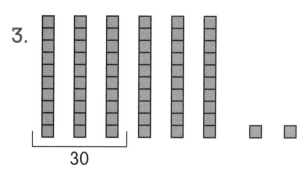

   30

   _____ cubes

Reading

Read. Then answer the question.

Every day after school, Dad gets us a snack. On Monday, we went to the fruit market and got apples. Today, Dad stopped in front of the ice cream shop.

4. What do you think will happen next? Tell why.

_____

_____

Language

Write the sentence correctly.

1. did you find it

   _____

   _____

2. i did not find it

   _____

   _____

Math

Use the number line to count on.

3.

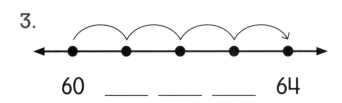

60 ____ ____ ____ 64

4.

65 ____ ____ 68 ____

Reading

Read. Then answer the question.

Sam likes the color blue. He likes to put on blue socks. He likes to put on blue shoes. One day, Sam's mom bought him new red shoes. "Your blue shoes have holes in them," said his mom.

5. What do you think Sam will do? Tell why.

_____

_____

_____

Language

Write the sentence correctly.

1. that is my toy

_____

_____

2. my mom gave it to me

_____

_____

Math

Count on to finish the chart. Write the numbers.

3.

70		72	
74			77
	79	80	
82			85

Reading

Read. Then answer the question.

One sunny day, Mr. Kemp took his dog to the park. Lucky saw all his dog friends. He started to jump up and down. He started to pull Mr. Kemp.

4. What do you think will happen next? Tell why.

_____

_____

_____

Language

To whom does it belong? Write to tell.

1. Sage's book is lost.

   Whose book is lost? _____

2. The doctor's door is closed.

   Whose door is closed? _____

Math

Read the problem. Count on to answer the question.

3. There are 85 pieces of cereal in the box. How many pieces of cereal are there in all?

85

_____ pieces of cereal in all

Reading

Read. Then answer the item.

Mr. Potter finished milking his cow. He put the milk cans in his wagon. He told his horse, "Giddy up, Bessie!" He stopped at each house to put milk cans on the steps. This was how people got their milk.

4. This story tells about something that would happen _____.

   ○ now   ○ long ago

Language

To whom does it belong? Write to tell.

1. Miss White's dress is red.

   Whose dress is red? _____

2. Mom's hair is long.

   Whose hair is long? _____

Math

Count on. Write all the numbers. Then write how many in all.

3.

90

__ __ __ __ __ __ __

_____ leaves in all

Reading

Read. Then answer the items.

Lucy rides the bus home after school.
She does her homework. She feeds her
pets. She watches TV. She plays outside.

4. This story tells about something that would happen _____.

   ○ now   ○ long ago

5. Circle the words that help you know.

Language

Write 's to show to whom it belongs.

1. My sister_____ cat is named Fluffy.

2. Fluffy_____ fur is soft and white.

3. My cat_____ name is Stripes.

Math

Count on. Write how many.

4.

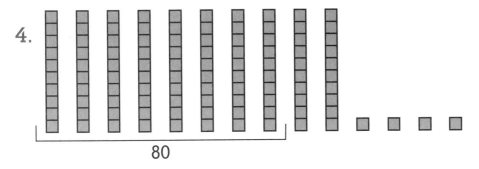

80

_____ cubes

Reading

Read. Then answer the question.

Wilma wants to see the monkeys. Her brother wants to see the hippos. "Okay, first we will see the monkeys, and then we will see the hippos. But after that, I want to see the lions," said Wilma's mom.

5. Where are the people in the story?

   ○ at a store   ○ at the zoo

Language

Write ('s) to show to whom or to what it belongs.

1. The man_____ hands are big.

2. Kaleb_____ tooth is loose.

3. The horse_____ tail is long.

Math

Use the number line to count on.

4.
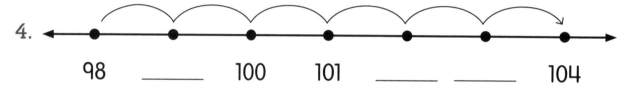

98 _____ 100 101 _____ _____ 104

5.
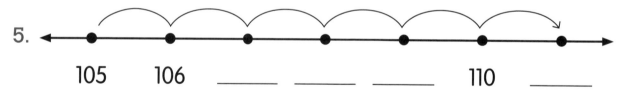

105 106 _____ _____ _____ 110 _____

Reading

Read. Then answer the items.

Mom and Dad set up the tent. I looked for small sticks for the fire. The yellow moon gave us light. I could see the tall trees all around us. An owl flew by.

6. Where are the people in the story?

○ at a campsite   ○ at home

7. Circle the words that help you know.

Name _____

Language

Write 's to show to whom it belongs. Then write to tell to whom it belongs.

1. This is his friend_____ bike.

   Whose bike is it? _____

2. Mom has Sara_____ coat.

   Whose coat is it? _____

Math

Count on to finish the chart. Write the numbers.

3.

101					106		108		110
			114				118		

Reading

Read. Then answer the items.

> The bell rang and the kids lined up. Mrs. Yang led us back to class. It was time for science. We each had one cup of water and one cup of sand.

4. Where are the people in the story?

   _____

5. Circle the words that help you know.

Name _____

Language

Write the word to take the place of the person.

1. Mom sits.

   _____ sits.
   He   She

2. Tyler plays the piano.

   _____ plays the piano.
   He   She

Math

Look at the problem. Use the picture to count on and add. Write the answer.

3. 6 + 4 = _____

Reading

Read. Then answer the item.

Mr. Lopez goes to the library every week. He gets 10 books to read. He reads books to the kids while he is there. On Thursdays, he reads books to the kids at the school by his house.

4. We know that Mr. Lopez _____.

   ○ likes to read

   ○ likes to walk

Language

Write the word to take the place of the animal.

1. A bee flies.

   _____ flies.

   She   **It**

2. A fish swims.

   _____ swims.

   He   **It**

Math

Look at the problem. Which number line can you use to find the answer?

3. 7 + 5 = __**?**__

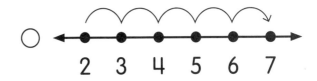

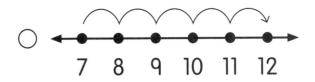

Reading

Read. Then answer the question.

It was the first day of school. Jordan did not want the summer to end. He liked to be at home with his mom. Jordan walked very slowly to his class. He did not see anyone he knew. He sat down and put his hands over his face.

4. How do you think Jordan is feeling? Tell why.

_____

_____

Name _____

Language

Write the word to take the place of the thing.

1. The book got wet.

   _____ got wet.

   He   It

2. The store is open.

   _____ is open.

   She   It

Math

Look at the number sentence. Use the diagram to count on and add. Write the answer.

3. 15 + 2 = _____

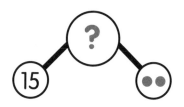

Reading

Read. Then answer the question.

"Kitty, where are you?" called Miss Green. She looked all around the house. She went next door and asked Mr. Evans if he had seen Kitty. "Not since last week," said Mr. Evans. Miss Green walked up and down the street calling, "Kitty! Kitty!"

4. What problem does Miss Green have?

_____

Language

Write the word to take the place of the underlined words.

1. <u>Suzi and I</u> run fast.

   _____ run fast.
   We   They

2. <u>Nick and Ben</u> cheer.

   _____ cheer.
   We   They

Math

Look at the number sentence. Use the number line to count on and add. Write the answer.

3. $21 + 4 =$ _____

21 22 23 24 25 26

Reading

Read. Then answer the question.

"I lost my dollar!" cried Brianna. Her older sister Mary put her arm around her and said, "Don't cry. I'll give you one of my dollars." Mary held Brianna's hand as they waited for the ice cream truck.

4. What do you know about Mary?

_____

Language

Write the word to take the place of the underlined words.

> He   She   It
> They   We

1. <u>Dad and I</u> fish.

   _____ fish.

2. <u>The boat</u> is big.

   _____ is big.

Math

Solve the problem. Draw counters, or dots, if you need them to count on.

3. 26 + 3 = _____

4. 30 + 7 = _____

Reading

Read. Then answer the questions.

Ryan put on a big red hat and made a funny face. Then he hopped around like a frog. He made all the kids laugh. Next, he told a joke and sang a silly song. The kids clapped.

5. What word tells about Ryan?

   ○ funny

   ○ quiet

6. What do you know about Ryan?

   _____

Language

Read the sentence. Is it correct? Mark **yes** or **no**.

1. The rabbit hops   ○ yes   ○ no

2. The rabbits hop.   ○ yes   ○ no

3. The boys read.   ○ yes   ○ no

4. The boys reads.   ○ yes   ○ no

Math

Count back. Write the numbers. Then pick the number that comes last.

Start here

5.

?								14	15

○ 16   ○ 6

Reading

Read. Then answer the item.

Planting a flower garden is easy.
First, you dig some holes in the dirt.
Next, you put flower seeds in the
holes. Then, you water the seeds
every day. Soon flowers will grow.

6. The author wrote this to _____.

○ tell a story   ○ tell how to do something

Language

Read the sentence. Is it correct? Mark **yes** or **no**.

1. The boy bakes. ○ yes ○ no

2. The boys bakes. ○ yes ○ no

3. The girls sleeps. ○ yes ○ no

4. The girl sleeps. ○ yes ○ no

Math

Count back. Write the numbers.

Start here

5.

		21		23			26		28

Reading

Read. Then answer the item.

Do you like apples? I do! Everyone should eat apples. Apples are good for you. If you eat an apple every day, you will feel great.

6. The author wrote this to _____.

○ get you to eat apples

○ make you smile

Language

Write the correct word to finish the sentence.

1. A _____ likes grass.

    cows   cow

2. The baby _____ milk.

    like   likes

Math

Count back. Write the numbers.

Start here

3.

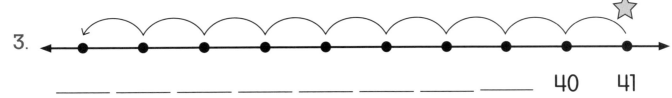

____ ____ ____ ____ ____ ____ ____ ____ 40 41

Reading

Read. Then answer the item.

> I have a new pet bunny. He is so funny. He hides in an old hat. He runs after my cat! He hops on my bed and sits on my head! I think I'll call him "funny bunny"!

4. The author wrote this to _____.

   ○ make you smile

   ○ tell you how to do something

Language

Write the correct word to finish the sentence.

1. Mom _____ lunch.
   make   **makes**

2. The _____ listen.
   kid   **kids**

Math

Count back. Write the numbers.

3.

Start here ☆

									50

Reading

Read. Then answer the item.

We can see the moon.
It is smaller than Earth.
The moon has no air.
No people or plants live there.

4. The author wrote this to _____.

   ○ get you to do something

   ○ tell you about something

Language

Draw a line to match. Then read the sentence.

1. My dad •   • like music.

2. The horses •   • goes to work.

3. Many people •   • go to the barn.

Math

Count back. Write the numbers.

4.

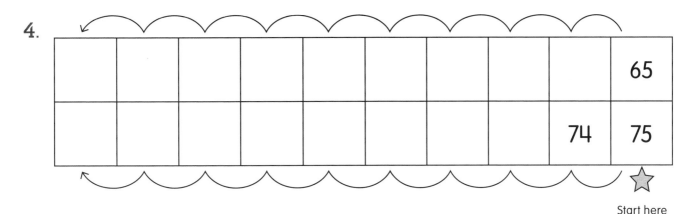

									65
								74	75

Start here

Reading

Read. Then answer the item.

Animals Grow and Change

A frog starts as an egg. It turns into a tadpole. Then it grows legs and its tail goes away. Now it is a frog.

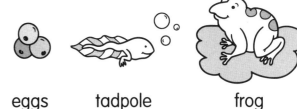

eggs   tadpole   frog

5. The author wrote this to _____.

   ○ get you to do something   ○ tell you something

Language

Write **is** or **are** to finish the sentence.

1. The park _____ a busy place.

2. There _____ many kids playing.

3. It _____ hot today.

4. They _____ leaving now.

Math

Look at the problem. Use the picture to count back and subtract. Write the answer.

5. $9 - 6 =$ _____

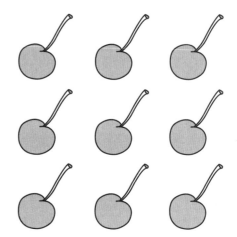

Reading

Read. Then answer the questions.

Have You Seen Me?

My name is Stan.
Last seen on Grove St.
**Please call 555-5555
if you find me.**

6. What is the poster about?

○ a bird for sale

○ a lost bird

○ a pet store

7. How do you know?

_____

_____

Language

Write **is** or **are** to finish the sentence.

1. Liz _____ my sister.

2. Farzin and Abir _____ my brothers.

3. My parents _____ coming home.

4. My grandpa _____ so much fun.

Math

Look at the problem. Which number line can you use to find the answer?

5. $13 - 4 =$ __?__

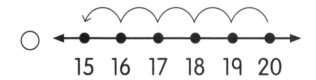

○ 9 10 11 12 13 14

○ 15 16 17 18 19 20

Reading

Read. Then answer the questions.

Fun Time Park put up this sign on its gate:

No Dogs

6. What is the sign at the park about?

○ a lost dog

○ dogs can go in

○ dogs cannot go in

7. How do you know?

_____

_____

Language

Write **was** or **were** to finish the sentence.

1. I _____ on the blue team last week.

2. Joe and Enzo _____ on the red team.

3. They _____ having fun.

4. It _____ almost dark.

Math

Look at the number sentence. Use the diagram to count back and subtract. Write the answer.

5. 16 – 2 = _____

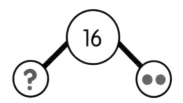

Reading

Read. Then answer the questions.

Class Rules
1. Listen
2. Follow directions
3. Raise your hand
4. Be kind
5. Help each other

6. Who are these rules for?
   ○ the kids
   ○ the teachers

7. Where are these rules posted?
   ○ at the park
   ○ at school

Language

Write **was** or **were** to finish the sentence.

1. Mom and Dad _____ singing.

2. Tony _____ clapping.

3. _____ he late?

4. _____ you there?

Math

Look at the number sentence. Use the number line to count back and subtract. Write the answer.

5. 23 − 6 = _____

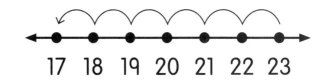

17 18 19 20 21 22 23

Reading

Read. Then answer the items.

Contents

Cookies...................... page 6

Cakes......................... page 26

Pies............................ page 46

6. What can you read about on page 26?

_____

7. The pictures are there to _____.

   ○ help me know more about the book

   ○ tell me the page numbers

Language

Write to finish the sentence.

| is | are | was | were |

1. This _____ Ali.

2. We _____ both six.

3. We _____ in the same class last year.

4. It _____ a fun year.

Math

Solve the problem. Draw counters, or dots, if you need them to count back.

5. $34 - 5 =$ _____

6. $38 - 3 =$ _____

Reading

Read. Then answer the questions.

For Sale

2 days only!
$49.00 at
We Like Bikes
345 Pine Street

7. What is for sale?

_____

8. How many days is the sale?

_____

Language

Write to tell to whom something belongs.

> his   hers   ours

1. Ron says those socks are _____.

2. Trish and I lost _____ yesterday.

Math

Is the number sentence true? Mark **yes** or **no**.

3. $8 = 8$ ○ yes   ○ no

4. $12 = 13$ ○ yes   ○ no

5. $7 = 16$ ○ yes   ○ no

Reading

Read. Then answer the question.

One day, a bear was looking for food to eat. She saw bees going into a log. "There is honey in that log," thought the bear. She broke open the log to get the honey. The bees were mad. The bear ran and jumped into a lake.

6. Why were the bees mad?

○ The bear tried to get their honey.   ○ The bear ran away.

Language

Write to tell to whom something belongs.

> theirs   yours   mine

1. My sisters made kites. Those kites are _____.

2. Our books look the same. Is that book _____ or _____?

Math

Is the number sentence true? Mark **yes** or **no**.

3. $9 = 8 + 1$ ○ yes   ○ no

4. $12 - 1 = 11$ ○ yes   ○ no

5. $6 = 3 + 5$ ○ yes   ○ no

Reading

Read. Then answer the item.

Boom, crash, ouch! Curtis fell off his bike. His arm hurt a lot! His mom took him to the doctor. Curtis had a broken arm!

6. Curtis's arm hurt a lot because ____.

   ○ his mom took him to the doctor   ○ he fell off his bike

Language

Write to tell to whom something belongs.

1. My mom is here. That van is _____.

   theirs   hers

2. That bag belongs to me. It is _____.

   mine   yours

Math

Is the number sentence true? Mark **yes** or **no**.

3. $10 - 5 = 2 + 3$ ◯ yes   ◯ no

4. $15 - 4 = 15 - 6$ ◯ yes   ◯ no

5. $1 + 9 = 9 + 1$ ◯ yes   ◯ no

Reading

Read. Then answer the question.

Three little kittens lost their mittens, and they began to cry. "Oh, mother dear, we sadly fear, our mittens we have lost."

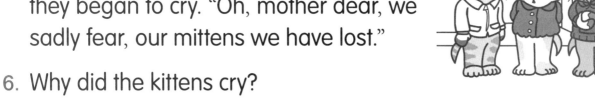

6. Why did the kittens cry?

_____

_____

Language

Write a sentence using the word (mine).

1. _____

Write a sentence using the word (theirs).

2. _____

Math

Is the number sentence true? Mark **yes** or **no**.

3. $14 - 5 = 8 + 2$ ⚪ yes ⚪ no

4. $5 + 18 = 18 + 5$ ⚪ yes ⚪ no

5. $16 + 1 = 19 - 2$ ⚪ yes ⚪ no

Reading

Read. Then answer the question.

Water can be a solid. When water gets very cold, it freezes, and it turns into a solid. Solid water is ice.

6. What happens when water gets very cold?

_____

Daily Fundamentals • EMC 3241 • © Evan-Moor Corp.

Language

Write a sentence using the word (**yours**).

1. _____

Write a sentence using the word (**ours**).

2. _____

Math

Read the word problem. Then answer the questions.

Sam ate 3 oranges, 1 apple, and 2 plums. Ben ate 3 figs, 2 pears, and 1 banana.

3. Did Sam and Ben eat the same number of fruits?   ○ yes   ○ no

4. How many fruits did each of them eat?   _____ fruits

Reading

Read. Then answer the question.

Your body gets energy from the foods you eat. You need energy to run, to play, and to do your work. If you eat good foods, your body will have a lot of energy.

5. How does your body get energy?

_____

Language

Look at the picture. Circle the correct word.

1.

   to

   two

2.

   flower

   flour

Math

Look at the number sentence. Use the model to find the unknown number. Write the number.

3. $7 +$ _____ $= 15$

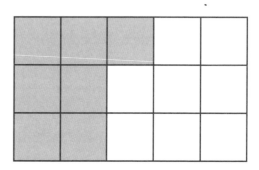

Reading

Read. Then answer the items.

Some birds fly south for the winter. They have to go where it is warm. Cats like to be warm. Birds find more bugs to eat in warm weather.

4. Cross out the sentence that doesn't belong.

5. Tell why.

_____

Language

Look at the picture. Circle the correct word.

1.  eight

ate

2.  night

knight

Math

Look at the number sentence. Use the model to find the unknown number. Write the number.

3. 18 – _____ = 12

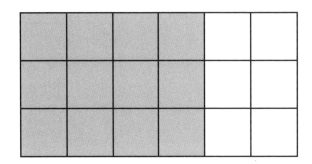

Reading

Read. Then answer the question.

Suzi had a loose tooth. Her brother put a string around it. He pulled the string, and the tooth came out! Now Suzi cannot eat apples.

4. What is the main idea?

○ Suzi had a loose tooth.

○ Suzi cannot eat apples.

Language

Match the picture to the correct word.

1. •   • son

2.  •   • one

3.  •   • sun

4. •   • won

Math

Look at the number sentence. Use the diagram to find the unknown number. Write the number.

5. $20 + \underline{\hspace{1cm}} = 29$

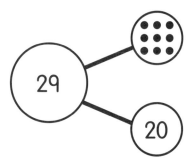

Reading

Read. Then answer the question.

I just got a new book. It is about elephants. I will find out what elephants eat. I will find out where elephants live. I will read my book today.

6. What is the main idea?

   ○ I will read my book today.

   ○ I just got a new book about elephants.

Language

Look at the picture. Circle the correct word.

1.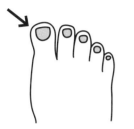

toe

tow

2.

pear

pair

Math

Look at the number sentence. Use the diagram to find the unknown number. Write the number.

3. 30 – _____ = 25

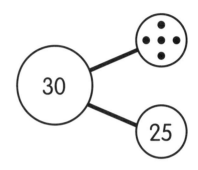

Reading

Read. Then answer the item.

> Dear Ann,
>   I have five new fish.
> Three fish are yellow with
> black stripes. Two fish
> are blue with yellow spots.
> I don't know what to name
> my new fish.
>
>   From,
>   Tyson

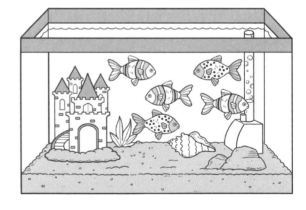

4. Draw a ⭕ next to the sentences that tell about Tyson's new fish.

Name _____

Language

Match the picture to the correct word.

1.  •   • sea

2.  •   • dear

3.  •   • see

4. [image] •   • deer

Math

Mark the number that makes the number sentence true.

5. $6 + \underline{\ ?\ } = 28$

   ○ 30   ○ 22

6. $20 - \underline{\ ?\ } = 11$

   ○ 9   ○ 11

Reading

Read. Then answer the question.

Some ants live in logs. They make their nests in wood. These ants are red or black, and they are big! Some logs have as many as 2,000 ants in them!

7. What is the main idea?

_____

Language

Look at the picture. Write the correct word.

1.  The dog is _____ the house.

                                             in   **near**

2.  They are _____ the umbrella.

                                       behind   **under**

Math

Read the word problem. Then mark the answer.

Granny made 4 vanilla cupcakes.
She also made 4 lemon cupcakes.
How many cupcakes did she make altogether?

3. To answer the question, you have to _____.

○ add   ○ subtract   ○ skip count

Reading

Read. Then answer the question.

Mr. Mateo looked at the peaches on the tree. He felt
them and looked at their color to see if they were ripe.
Then he got a basket and started picking them off the tree.

4. What does **ripe** mean?

○ ready   ○ big

Language

Look at the picture. Write the correct word.

1.  Jim sits _____ the bench.

on   near

2.  Link sits _____ the tree.

behind   under

Math

Read the word problem. Then mark the answer.

Tyrone had 10 grapes in a bowl.
Then he ate 7 of them.
How many grapes does he have left?

3. To answer the question, you have to _____.

○ add   ○ subtract   ○ skip count

Reading

Read. Then answer the question.

Elsa borrowed four books from the library. She had to return them in one week. "I'd better start reading these right away!" she said to herself.

4. What does the word **return** mean?

○ to give away   ○ to give back

Name _____

Language

Look at the picture. Write the correct word.

1. 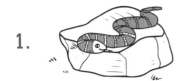 The snake is _____ the rock.

on   in

2.  The mouse is _____ the shoes.

between   under

Math

Read the word problem. Then mark the answer.

Burt saw 6 white trucks.
Then he saw 5 gray trucks.
How many trucks did he see altogether?

3. Mark the number sentence that tells about the problem.

○ 6 – 5 = ?   ○ 6 + 5 = ?   ○ 6 + ? = 5

Reading

Read. Then answer the question.

Joe and Tim were best friends. Joe let Tim borrow his favorite video game. "I'll be careful with it," Tim promised. "I know you will," said Joe. "I trust you."

4. What does the word **borrow** mean?

○ to use something of someone else's and keep it

○ to use something of someone else's then give it back

Language

Look at the picture. Write the correct word.

1.  The crab is _____ the rock.
behind   under

2.  The mouse is _____ the cheese.
between   near

Math

Read the word problem. Then mark the answer.

The tree had 16 coconuts growing on it.
Then 9 coconuts fell to the ground.
How many coconuts were left on the tree?

3. Mark the number sentence that tells about the problem.

○ 16 + ? = 9   ○ 16 + 9 = ?   ○ 16 − 9 = ?

Reading

Read. Then answer the question.

Josh loved to draw pictures of animals. Every day after school he would draw. But one day, he could not find his markers. He looked everywhere, but he did not find them. His mom saw him sitting on his bed and asked him, "Why do you look so glum, Josh?"

4. What does the word **glum** mean?
○ happy   ○ unhappy

Daily Fundamentals • EMC 3241 • © Evan-Moor Corp.

Language

Write sentences about the picture. Use the words **under** and **on**.

1. _____

_____

_____

Math

Read the word problem. Then mark the answer.

Kelly's coat had 18 buttons.
Then 4 buttons fell off.
How many buttons were left on the coat?

2. Mark the number sentence that tells about the problem.

○ 18 − 4 = ?   ○ 18 + 4 = ?   ○ 18 + ? = 4

Reading

Read. Then answer the question.

Grandpa and I went to the zoo today. I ran outside as soon as I saw Grandpa's car. "Fasten your seatbelt," said Grandpa. "Safety first," I said as I pulled the strap across me and heard the buckle click. "Now let's go see the lions!" I said.

3. What does the word **fasten** mean?
○ lock   ○ pull

Language

Read the sentence. Circle the word that tells how something **smells**.

1. The trash smells stinky!

2. The house smells clean.

3. The cookie smells sweet.

4. The blanket smells old.

Math

Read the word problem. Draw a picture to solve it. Write the answer.

5. Ted has 7 white plates. He also has 6 blue plates. How many plates does he have altogether?

_____ plates

Reading

Read. Then answer the question.

Have you been to see a movie at a theater? Movies have different prices at different times. If you see a movie during the day, it will cost you $5.00. If you see a movie at night, it will cost you $7.00.

6. Which sentence summarizes the text?

○ Movies cost less during the day than at night.

○ You can see a movie during the day or at night.

Daily Fundamentals • EMC 3241 • © Evan-Moor Corp.

Language

Read the sentence. Circle the word that tells about **shape**.

1. That is a round table.

2. My book is square.

3. The pancake is flat.

4. The banana is crooked.

Math

Read the word problem. Draw a picture to solve it. Write the answer.

5. Anna had 14 pens. Then she lost 5 of them. How many pens does she have left?

_____ pens

Reading

Read. Then answer the question.

The day is icy. The day is cold. Kate will go skate. She skips to the gate. She sits down and puts on her skates. She sees the ice is as smooth as a dinner plate. Kate begins to skate.

6. Which sentence summarizes the text?

○ Kate went through a gate to skate.

○ Kate went to skate on a cold and icy day.

Language

Read the sentence. Circle the word that tells how something **sounds**.

1. The music is loud.

2. The quiet baby sleeps.

3. The noisy kids played.

4. The woman has a soft voice.

Math

Read the word problem. Then answer the item.

Dan washed 8 cups and 7 spoons. How many things did Dan wash altogether?

5. Write a number sentence to solve the problem. Write the answer after the =.

_____

Reading

Read. Then answer the question.

Nikki's new shoes felt good. She wiggled her toes inside the comfy blue shoes. Nikki had spent all her birthday money to buy them. She had been wanting them for two months! Nikki tied her yellow laces in big bows and ran out the door to school.

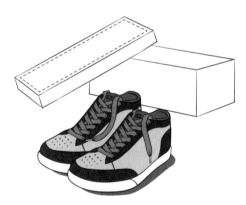

6. Which sentence summarizes the text?

○ Nikki just got the shoes with yellow laces that she had been wanting.

○ Nikki wore her blue and yellow shoes to school.

Language

Read the sentence. Circle the word that tells how something **tastes**.

1. The chips taste salty.

2. The sweet cake is good.

3. The grapes are too sour.

4. The tamale is yummy.

Math

Read the word problem. Then answer the item.

There were 16 ducks at the pond. Then 5 of them flew away. How many ducks were left at the pond?

5. Write a number sentence to solve the problem. Write the answer after the =.

_____

Reading

Read. Then answer the question.

We use tools to help us know more about the weather. A thermometer shows us how hot or cold the air is. A wind vane shows which direction the wind is blowing. A rain gauge tells us how much rain fell. You may have seen weather tools outside your house.

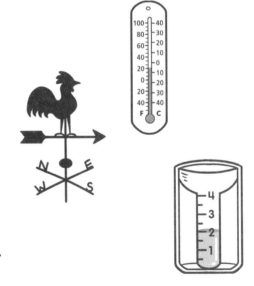

6. Which sentence summarizes the text?

○ Weather tools such as thermometers, wind vanes, and rain gauges help us know more about the weather.

○ Weather tools such as a thermometer go outside your home.

Language

Write the best word to finish the sentence.

clean   sweet   flat   loud

1. My hands smell _____.

2. The car is _____.

3. The box is _____.

4. The pie is _____.

Math

Read the word problem.
Write the answer.

5. The park has 12 apple trees, 3 pear trees, and 5 plum trees. How many trees does the park have?

_____ trees

Reading

Read. Then answer the question.

Wood is used to make many things. Some tables are made of wood. Some chairs are made of wood. Did you know that paper is made from wood? Special tools and machines help make wood into many things.

6. Which sentence summarizes the text?

   ○ Special tools and machines are used to make things.

   ○ Wood can be made into many things, such as tables, chairs, and paper.

Language

Read the sentence. It is missing commas.
Write a comma between things in a list.

1. Jeff has an apple chips and a drink.

2. Mr. Lays has to sweep dust and wash.

3. The little girl saw a lion a bear and a fox.

Math

Look at the number. Draw a line from the number to its model.

4. 40 •

5. 50 •

6. 10 •

7. 60 •

Reading

Read. Then answer the question.

"Beep!" went the big truck as it sped by Mr. Smith's shoe store. Mr. Smith looked outside his store window and saw cars and trucks zoom by. The streets were crowded with people carrying bags. Kids stood on the corner waiting to cross the busy street.

8. Where is Mr. Smith's shop?

○ in the city   ○ in the country

Language

Read the sentence. It is missing commas.
Write a comma between things in a list.

1. There will be balloons candy and music.

2. The boys saw red blue and green bikes.

3. Mrs. Meyer likes the colors blue pink and red.

Math

Look at the model. Write the number that tells how many.

4.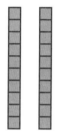

5.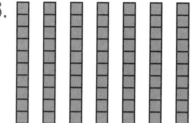

6.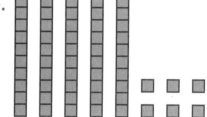

_____   _____   _____

Reading

Read. Then answer the question.

This week, the first grade students will plant flowers in front of the school. Last week, the second grade students planted trees in front of the school. The week before that, the third grade students painted the front steps. Next week, the fourth grade students will paint the front doors of the school.

7. Why do you think the students are doing these things?

_____

 Daily Fundamentals • EMC 3241 • © Evan-Moor Corp.

Name _____

Language

Read the sentence. It is missing commas. Rewrite the sentence using commas.

1. I look like my mom my sister and my brother.

_____

2. My dad has red hair blue eyes and big ears.

_____

Math

Look at the number. Draw a model that shows how many.

3. 30

4. 10

5. 63

Reading

Read. Then answer the questions.

Mrs. White put a book on every desk. Then she wrote the homework on the board. After that she looked for a Halloween art project. Ten minutes later the bell rang, and it was time for Mrs. White to go to the playground.

6. What is Mrs. White's job? _____

7. What words helped you know? _____

Language

Read the sentence. It is missing commas. Rewrite the sentence using commas.

1. I like to learn about animals space and cars.

_____

2. My dog has brown fur a pink nose and white feet.

_____

Math

Finish the chart. Write how many tens and ones.

Number	Model	Tens	Ones
3. 82			
4. 25			

Reading

Read. Then answer the items.

Fuyu put on her warm boots and heavy coat. She looked around her room for her gloves and her hat. She found them drying on her bench. She put those on, as well. Then she stopped by the front door to get her sled before she went outside.

5. What do you think the weather is like outside?

_____

6. Tell why you think so. _____

Language

Write three things you ate today.
Write a comma between each thing.

1. _____

_____

Math

Finish the chart. Write how many or draw a model.

Number	Model	Tens	Ones
2.			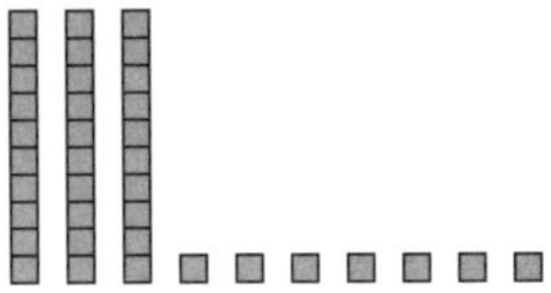 7
3. 94			

Reading

Read. Then answer the items.

Dad put the suitcases in the trunk of the car. Mom put the pillows and blankets in the back seat. I brought books and my tablet. Mom says that we can stop for food along the way. I just hope I can sleep for part of it.

4. What do you think this family is doing?

_____

5. Underline the words or sentences that helped you know.

Language

Read the sentences. Then write the word that tells **how** the action happened.

1. The music played loudly.
   How did the music play?

   _____

2. The man walked slowly.
   How did the man walk?

   _____

Math

Look at the number. Write 10 more.

3.
20

5.
14

4.
35

6.
51

Reading

Read. Then answer the questions.

Have you ever made cookies? First, you turn on the oven. Then, you mix the flour, salt, and sugar. Next, put in the eggs and vanilla and mix everything together. Finally, drop spoonfuls of dough onto a tray. Last, put the tray into the oven.

7. What is the first thing you do?

_____

8. What is the last thing you do?

_____

Language

Read the sentences. Then write the word that tells **when** the action happened.

1. I go to school tomorrow.
   When do I go to school?

   _____

2. Tracy should leave now.
   When should Tracy leave?

   _____

Math

Look at the number. Write 10 less.

3. [90]

4. [39]

5. [50]

6. [83]

Reading

Read. Then answer the item.

We live in Aspen, Colorado. During the winter it snows a lot. Before Dad can take me to school, he has to shovel the snow off of the driveway. Then, he starts the car to warm it up. Next, he gets the snow off of the glass. Finally, we get in the car to go to school.

7. Write **1**, **2**, **3**, **4** to tell what happened.

   _____ get in the car to go to school

   _____ starts the car to warm it up

   _____ gets the snow off of the glass

   _____ shovel the snow off of the driveway

Language

Read the sentence. Circle the word that tells **where** the action happens.

1. Seals swim nearby.

2. A crab swims away.

3. I see fish everywhere.

4. The turtle hides inside.

Math

Look at the number. Write ten more and ten less.

5.

less		more
	46	

6.

less		more
	87	

Reading

Read. Then answer the items.

Can It Be Fixed?

1. Nico's dad fixed his toy.
2. Nico's toy broke.
3. Nico asked his dad to fix his toy.
4. Now Nico can play with his toy again.

7. Is this story in the right order?

  ○ yes   ○ no

8. Tell why.

_____

_____

Language

Write **ly** to make the word an adverb. Then read the sentence.

1. Diana cuts careful_____.

2. Scott writes neat_____.

3. Kim walks slow_____.

4. Ben moves quick_____.

Math

Read the word problem. Write the answer.

5. Josh tried to buy 24 donuts, but the shop clerk gave him 10 extra donuts. How many donuts did Josh get altogether?

_____ donuts

Reading

Read. Then answer the questions.

Mrs. Davis helps at the zoo every Friday. The monkeys are really hungry in the morning, so Mrs. Davis feeds them first. The hippos wake up early, so Mrs. Davis feeds them next. Then, she feeds the giraffes. The big cats are the last to be fed.

6. Which animals does Mrs. Davis feed second?

_____

7. Which animals does Mrs. Davis feed after she feeds the giraffes?

_____

Language

Write **ly** to make the word an adverb. Then read the sentence.

1. The men cheered loud_____.

2. The boy rides quick_____.

Write an adverb.

3. _____

Math

Read the word problem. Write the answer.

4. Beth had 65 pieces of paper in her backpack. Then she gave 10 pieces to her sister. How many pieces of paper does Beth have left in her backpack?

_____ pieces of paper

Reading

Read. Then answer the questions.

Babies learn to do a lot of things before they are two years old. First, they learn to crawl. Second, they learn to walk. Third, they learn to run.

5. Which three words tell you the order that things happen?

_____

6. Is the order important?

○ yes   ○ no

Language

Circle the part of the sentence that tells
who or **what** the sentence talks about.

1. The class worked at their desks.

2. The teacher rang the bell.

3. The fish swam in their bowl.

Math

Look at each number and the model below it. Then write <, =, or >
in the ( ) to make a true number sentence.

4. 42 ( ) 42

5. 75 ( ) 67

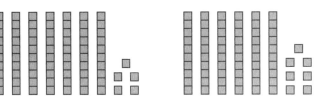

Reading

Read. Then answer the question.

Giraffes and elephants are both tall animals. A giraffe has
a long neck. An elephant has a long trunk. A giraffe can
use its neck to eat leaves at the top of a tree. An elephant
uses its truck to get water from a river.

6. How are giraffes and elephants different?

   ○ Giraffes have long necks, and elephants have long trunks.

   ○ Giraffes and elephants are both tall animals.

Language

Circle the part of the sentence that tells **who** or **what** the sentence talks about.

1. The people lined up for the ride.

2. Many children laughed and smiled.

3. The small monkey danced a jig.

Math

Write <, =, or > in the ◯ to make a true number sentence.

4. 17 ◯ 23

6. 36 ◯ 36

5. 84 ◯ 48

7. 53 ◯ 54

Reading

Read. Then answer the question.

Have you ever gone on a trip to a place that is far from your home? Some people ride planes or trains when they travel. Both trains and planes can fit a lot of people. Trains travel on land. Planes travel by air. Both planes and trains have wheels.

8. How are planes and trains the same?

○ They both travel by land and air.

○ They both have wheels, and they both can fit a lot of people.

Language

Circle the part of the sentence that tells **what happens**.

1. My friend Will lost his tooth.

2. The baker made cookies.

3. The man helped a cat.

Math

Look at the number sentence. Then mark the number that will make it true.

4. 33 = __?__   ○ 33   ○ 59

5. 12 > __?__   ○ 11   ○ 21

6. 70 < __?__   ○ 68   ○ 73

Reading

Read. Then answer the item.

Plants and animals live in oceans.
Plants and animals also live in deserts.
Oceans are wet. Deserts are dry. But
both oceans and deserts have sand.

7. Underline the sentences that tell how oceans and deserts are the same.

Language

Circle the part of the sentence that tells **what happens**.

1. Lisa always wakes up at 7 a.m.

2. The police officer rides a bike.

3. Blanca likes to color.

Math

Look at the number sentence. Write a two-digit number to complete it.

4. $89 < \underline{\quad\quad}$

5. $45 = \underline{\quad\quad}$

6. $13 > \underline{\quad\quad}$

7. $60 > \underline{\quad\quad}$

8. $52 < \underline{\quad\quad}$

9. $99 = \underline{\quad\quad}$

Reading

Read. Then answer the items.

> Tran and his sister Lan do not go to bed at the same time.
> Tran is older than Lan. But both Tran and Lan brush their
> teeth and wash their face and hands before bed. Both of
> them also kiss their parents before bed.

10. Underline the sentences that tell how Tran and Lan are different.

11. Draw a ◯ next to the sentences that tell how they are the same.

Language

Write the part of the sentence that tells **what happens**.

1. Yesterday Ann _____.

2. Today Tom will _____.

3. Tomorrow Logan _____.

Math

Read the word problem. Then answer the items.

> Toya can sing 48 songs. Eddie can sing 51 songs.
> Who can sing more songs?

4. Who can sing more songs? _____

5. Write a number sentence about the problem. Use **<**, **=**, or **>**.

_____

Reading

Read. Then answer the items.

> Tori is going to a new school this year. Her old school had 300
> students. Her new school only has 100 students. Both schools have
> art classes. Both schools have a fall festival. Tori misses her old
> school, but she likes her new school more every day.

6. How are Tori's old school and new school the same?

_____

7. Underline the sentences that tell how the schools are different.

Language

Write a contraction from the word box to take the place of the two words.

> didn't   I'd

1. _____ be careful.
   I would

2. You _____ call me.
   did not

Math

Add. Look at the models.

3. 50 + 40 = _____

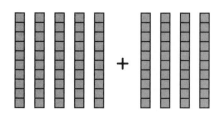

4. 60 + 20 = _____

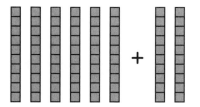

Reading

Read. Then answer the items.

A loud noise woke me up this morning. I looked out my window and saw a small squirrel carrying a big oak tree across the grass. "Hey!" I shouted, "Bring that back!" But the squirrel looked at me and kept on going.

5. This is about something _____.

   ○ real   ○ make-believe

6. Tell how you know.

   _____

Language

Write a contraction from the word box to take the place of the two words.

can't   you'll

1. I hope _____ have fun.
   you will

2. I _____ be late.
   can not

Math

Add. Look at the models.

3. 38 + 16 = _____

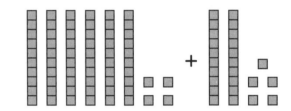

4. 64 + 25 = _____

Reading

Read. Then answer the question.

My cat Rufus always knows when I'm feeling sad. Yesterday when I got home from school, Rufus sat on my lap. When it was time for me to go to baseball practice, Rufus sat by the front window and watched me drive away.

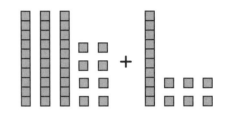

5. Is this story real or make-believe? Tell how you know.

_____

_____

Language

Write a contraction from the word box to take the place of the two words.

aren't   shouldn't

1. You _____ do that.
   should not

2. The kittens _____ sleeping.
   are not

Math

Add. Draw a model if you need it.

3. 32 + 27 = _____

4. 58 + 20 = _____

Reading

Read. Then answer the question.

My soccer coach is really nice. She teaches us a lot of different ways to kick the ball. She also helps us think about the rules while we play the game. I like when she shows us how to hit the soccer ball with our heads.

5. Is this story about something real or make-believe? Tell how you know.

_____

_____

Daily Fundamentals • EMC 3241 • © Evan-Moor Corp.

Language

Read the words. Write the contraction that goes with them.

> I'll   he's   couldn't

1. could not _____

2. he is _____

3. I will _____

Math

Add.

4. $46 + 39 =$ _____

5. $80 + 13 =$ _____

6. $71 + 24 =$ _____

7. $29 + 40 =$ _____

8. $50 + 50 =$ _____

9. $70 + 5 =$ _____

Reading

Read. Then answer the questions.

Freddy Fish got into his car and sped over to Sam Seal's house. "It's happening!" yelled Freddy Fish. "What's happening?" asked Sam Seal. "The whales are coming here to feed! They'll eat everything!" said a worried Freddy Fish.

10. What part of this story could be real?

_____

11. What part of the story could not be real?

_____

Language

Read the words. Write the contraction that goes with them.

| didn't | she'll | I'd |

1. she will _____

2. did not _____

3. I would _____

Math

Read the word problem. Add. Write the answer.

4. Mom put 49 peas in the pot of soup. Then Dad added 50 peas to the pot. How many peas are in the pot of soup altogether?

_____ peas

Reading

Read. Then answer the questions.

The Muri family eats dinner at 5:00 p.m. every night. Walter does not like to eat vegetables. But his parents say that if he eats all of his dinner, he can have dessert. Walter closed his eyes and ate his last string bean. "Okay, I'm ready for dessert," said Walter. Mrs. Muri snapped her fingers, and a bowl of ice cream appeared in front of Walter.

5. What part of this story could be real?

_____

6. What part of the story could not be real?

_____

Daily Fundamentals • EMC 3241 • © Evan-Moor Corp.

Language

Write the best word to finish the sentence.

and   but   so

1. I like the rain, _____ I don't like to be cold.

2. Tomorrow I will play _____ read a book.

Math

Look at the hour hand, or short hand, on the clock. Write the time.

3.

_____ : 00

4.

_____ : 00

5.

_____ : 00

Reading

Read. Then answer the question.

On Wednesdays Dillon goes next door to see if his neighbor Mrs. Dolson needs help. Sometimes he takes out the garbage for her. Sometimes he feeds her cat. This week Mrs. Dolson told Dillon that a family with kids moved in across the street. Dillon went over right away to see if they needed any help.

6. What do you know about Dillon?

_____

Language

Write the best word to finish the sentence.

because   or   so

1. I feel cold, _____ I will put on a coat.

2. I went to bed early _____ I was tired.

Math

Look at the clock. Mark the time.

3.  ○ 5:00   ○ 4:00

4. 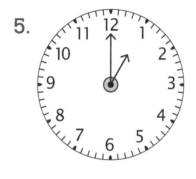 ○ 10:00   ○ 3:00

5. ○ 6:00   ○ 1:00

Reading

Read. Then answer the question.

Kara was not sure where she left her backpack. She looked in her room. She looked in the car. She could not find it. Kara thought maybe she left it across the street at Megan's house. Kara decided to put on her shoes and go to Megan's house, only her shoes were not in her room. They were not by the front door, either. Where were they?

6. What problem does Kara have?

Language

Make these two sentences into one sentence.
Use the word **and** in your sentence.

1. I like grapes. I like oranges.

_____

_____

Math

Look at the clock. Write the time.

2.

_____ : 30

3.

_____ : 30

4.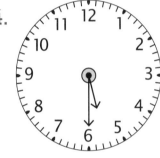

_____ : 30

Reading

Read. Then answer the question.

The ground was covered with snow, and the air was cool and crisp. Deshi sang to himself as he shoveled snow. He smiled and waved to his neighbors as they drove by. "Today is a beautiful day," he thought to himself.

5. How do you think Deshi is feeling? Tell how you know.

_____

_____

Language

Make these two sentences into one sentence.
Use the word **or** in your sentence.

1. Do you want milk? Do you want water?

_____

_____

Math

Look at the clock. Mark the time.

2.

  ○ 12:30   ○ 4:30

3.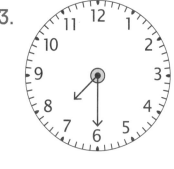

  ○ 7:30   ○ 3:30

4.

  ○ 11:30   ○ 10:30

Reading

Read. Then answer the item.

Yadira and Tabia are sisters. Yadira likes animals, and Tabia does not. "Get that cat out of our room!" shouted Tabia. Yadira quickly picked up her cat and closed the door. She let a tear drip down her cheek as she petted her cat. Suddenly, Tabia opened the door and threw the cat toys into the hall.

5. Mark the words that tell about Tabia.

☐ mean   ☐ helpful   ☐ bossy   ☐ caring

Language

Make these two sentences into one sentence.
Use the word **but** in your sentence.

1. I want to buy that. I don't have any money.

_____

_____

Math

Write the time. Remember to use a **:** in the time.

2.

_____

3.

_____

4.

_____

Reading

Read. Then answer the item.

Jayla took the five dollar bill out of her pocket as soon as she saw Ian coming. He had dropped it yesterday, and she could not catch up with him in time to tell him. "Here, Ian, you dropped this yesterday," said Jayla as she handed him the money.

5. Mark the words that tell about Jayla.

☐ selfish   ☐ honest   ☐ kind   ☐ mean

Language

Draw a line to match the words that have almost the **same** meaning.

1. big •   • small

2. tiny •   • jump

3. mad •   • huge

4. hop •   • angry

Math

Draw a line. Match the coin with its name and value.

5. [penny coin] •   • dime, 10¢

6. [nickel coin] •   • nickel, 5¢

7. [dime coin] •   • penny, 1¢

Reading

Read. Then answer the items.

Rat was at home snug in bed when he heard a scary sound. He called his friend Bug. "I'm scared," said Rat. "Can I come over?" Bug said yes, so Rat put on his coat and went to sleep at Bug's house. But they could not sleep, so they watched TV.

8. Does this story happen in one place?

   ○ yes   ○ no

9. Draw a line under the words that help you know.

Daily Fundamentals • EMC 3241 • © Evan-Moor Corp.

Language

Draw a line to match the words that have almost the **same** meaning.

1. begin •   • rush

2. happy •   • start

3. hurry •   • close

4. shut •   • glad

Math

Draw a line. Match the coin with its name and value.

5. •   • quarter, 25¢

6. •   • dime, 10¢

7. •   • nickel, 5¢

Reading

Read. Then answer the items.

Reya had a really fun year. In the summer, she played in the water. In the fall, she jumped in the leaves. In the winter, she made snowmen. In the spring, she flew her kite.

8. Does this story happen at one time?

   ○ yes   ○ no

9. Circle the words that help you know.

Language

Draw a line to match the words that have **opposite** meanings.

1. big •   • fast

2. slow •   • close

3. happy •   • little

4. open •   • sad

Math

Write the coin's name and value in cents. Remember to use ¢ after the number.

5.   name: _____

   value: _____

6.   name: _____

   value: _____

Reading

Read. Then answer the items.

Jackie sold her cow for some magic beans. She planted the beans outside her window. The next day, she saw a giant beanstalk outside her window. Up, up, up she climbed to the top of the beanstalk.

7. How much time passes in this story?

   ○ one hour   ○ one day

8. Draw a line under the words that help you know.

Language

Draw a line to match the words that have **opposite** meanings.

1. wet •   • hard

2. less •   • dry

3. up •   • down

4. soft •   • more

Math

Write the coin's name and value in cents. Remember to use ¢ after the number.

5. name: _____

value: _____

6. name: _____

value: _____

Reading

Read. Then answer the items.

   Betsy felt cold. She put her hand against the straw walls. She felt the wind blowing. Her papa had used straw and clay to build their small home. The dirt floor felt soft, but cold. She lit a small fire in the big black kettle to warm her hands.

7. This story is about something that would happen _____.

   ○ now   ○ long ago

8. Draw a line under the words that help you know.

Language

Write the word to complete the sentence.

1. **Hot** is the opposite of

   _____.

2. **Little** is almost the same

   as _____.

3. **Dark** is the opposite of

   _____.

Math

Count the group of coins. Write the value of the group in cents.

4.

   value: _____

5.

   value: _____

Reading

Read. Then answer the questions.

Clara and Joy were selling cookies. They wanted to use the money to buy winter coats for children who needed them. "Cookies for sale!" they called to the people coming out of the store. They set up their cookie stand outside a different store each week. In just three weeks, they made enough money to buy ten coats.

6. Where does this story happen? Tell how you know.

   _____

   _____

7. Does this story happen at one time? Tell how you know.

   _____

Name _____

Language

Write **er** to finish the sentence.

1.  Your legs are long_____ than mine.

2.  I am old_____ than my sister Kate.

3.  A rabbit moves fast_____ than a turtle.

Math

Circle the longer object in the pair.

4.

5.

6.

7.

Reading

Read. Then answer the question.

When Bina walked into her classroom, she saw that
each student had brought food to share. "Oh, no!
I forgot the grapes for the class party!" Bina thought.
Bina asked her teacher if she could call her mom.

8. What do you think will happen next?

_____

_____

Language

Write **est** to finish the sentence.

1. Ed is taller than Doug. Tim is the tall_____ of all.

2. A hippo is bigger than a lion. An elephant is the bigg_____ of all.

3. Florida is hotter than California. Texas is the hott_____ of all.

Math

Circle the shorter object in the pair.

4.

5.

6.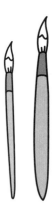

Reading

Read. Then answer the question.

> Lucy's Dog Wash Shop was filled with dirty dogs. "We have too many dogs to wash!" said Lucy. "I'd better put up the **closed** sign," said the head dog washer, Tim. Just as Tim was walking toward the door, a very tall woman with three small dogs walked into the shop.

7. What do you think Tim will do? Tell why.

_____

Language

Write **er** or **est** to finish the sentence.

1. That was the short_____ book I ever read!

2. This winter is cold_____ than last winter.

3. I am the old_____ child in my family.

Math

Put the objects in order from shortest to longest.
Write **1**, **2**, or **3** to tell the order.

4.

_____   _____   _____

5.

_____   _____   _____

Reading

Read. Then answer the question.

Selma Wynn loved to bake pies. Today she would make a cherry pie. She made the dough. Then she discovered she did not have any cherries. She looked everywhere, but all she found were apples.

6. What do you predict Selma Wynn will do? Tell why.

_____

_____

Language

Write **er** or **est** to finish the sentence.

1. I am smart_____ this year than I was last year.

2. This is the dark_____ night we've had.

3. The deep_____ part of the pool is 7 feet.

Math

Look at the group of objects. Then mark the answer.

4. The _____ is the longest.
   - ○ pencil
   - ○ lizard

5. The _____ is the shortest.
   - ○ pencil
   - ○ hairbrush

Reading

Read. Then answer the question.

Mrs. Miller plans one art project for her class to do each week. Today her class will paint pictures of pumpkins. Next week, they will paint pictures of black cats. As Mrs. Miller sets up for the art project, she sees that she does not have any orange paint.

6. What do you predict Mrs. Miller will do? Tell why.

_____

_____

Language

Write the best word to finish the sentence.

> harder   quickest   colder

1. Long words are _____ to spell than short words.

2. Yesterday was cold, but today is _____.

Math

Look at the group of objects. Read the sentences. Then write the answer.

3. Look at the stick and the straw. Which is longer? _____

4. Look at the leaf and the stick. Which is longer? _____

5. Which is longer, the leaf or the straw? _____

Reading

Read. Then answer the question.

Tyler cheered and waved as the parade went by. It was 11:30 a.m. when he saw the first cloud in the sky and felt a few wet drops. Some people said, "It's going to rain," and they left. As the band marched by, rain came pouring down from the sky.

6. What do you predict will happen next? Tell why.

_____

_____

Language

Add **.** or **?** to make it a sentence.

1. Where are my shoes_____

2. Today is Friday_____

3. Have you seen Lucy_____

4. I like ice cream_____

Math

Use the cubes to measure the object. Write the length.

5.

_____ cubes long

6.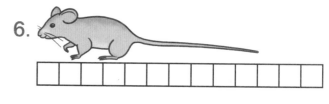

_____ cubes long

Reading

Read. Then answer the item.

Rita Raccoon had been in every garbage can on Pine Avenue looking for a pizza. So far, all she had found was half a donut—yum— and a corn dog—yum again. Rita wondered if her brother Ricky was having any luck on Maple Street. She hoped so, because it was Pizza Friday at their house.

7. The author wrote this to _____.

○ get you to eat pizza

○ make you smile

Language

Add ! or ? to make it a sentence.

1. Watch out for the ball_____

2. How are you_____

3. That's cool_____

4. I said stop that_____

Math

Use the cubes to measure the object. Write the length.

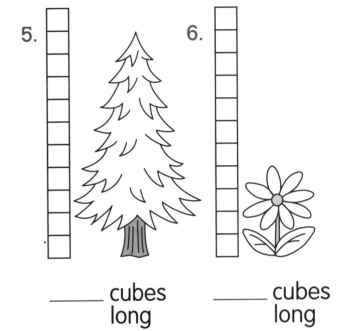

5. _____ cubes long

6. _____ cubes long

Reading

Read. Then answer the items.

Most kids like to eat fruit. Bananas, oranges, grapes, and plums are all fruits. I like bananas best. If you haven't tried a banana, you should. They are soft and sweet. You can use bananas to make a peanut butter and banana sandwich.

7. The author wrote this to _____.

   ○ get you to eat bananas

   ○ make you smile

8. Did it make you smile? _____

Language

Add ! or ? to make it a sentence.

1. Hey, that's mine_____

2. Do you know Alicia_____

3. I'm tired now_____

4. Are you ready to go_____

Math

Look at the raisins to measure the object. Write the length.

5.
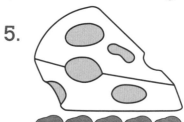

_____ raisins long

6.

_____ raisins long

Reading

Read. Then answer the question.

What's white and black and furry all over? A giant panda bear. These 300-pound bears are found in the mountains in China. A giant panda's favorite food is bamboo. In fact, most giant pandas eat bamboo 12 hours a day.

7. Why do you think the author wrote this?

_____

_____

Language

Write a sentence that asks a **question**. Use  .

1. _____

   _____

Write a sentence that tells someone to do something. Use ❗ .

2. _____

   _____

Math

Look at the raisins to measure the object. Write the length.

3.

_____ raisins long

4.

_____ raisins long

Reading

Read. Then answer the question.

My Little Sister

My little sister is a funny girl. She likes to hop, skip, and twirl. When she touches her nose to her toes, she says her hair grows! When she plays with our cat, she wears it like a hat! My mom and dad just laugh and say, "Well, how about that!"

5. Why do you think the author wrote this?

_____

Language

Write a sentence that asks a question.

1. _____

_____

Write a sentence that tells someone you are very excited about something.

2. _____

_____

Math

Draw an object that is 6 cubes long.

3.

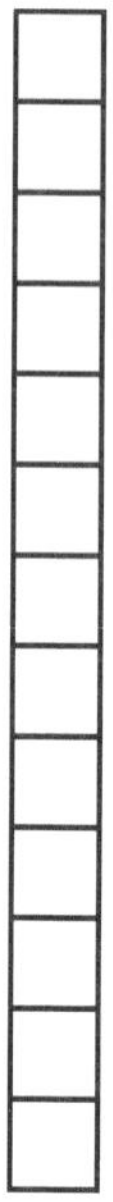

Reading

Read. Then answer the question.

More people should swim. Swimming is really fun. It is also good for your body. Being in the water on a hot day really helps cool you off. Swimming laps and playing in the water is a great way to get some exercise. If you haven't tried swimming, you really should. I bet you will like it!

4. Why do you think the author wrote this?

_____

_____

Daily Fundamentals • EMC 3241 • © Evan-Moor Corp.

Language

Read the sentence. Circle the compound word.

1. I see a rainbow in the sky.

2. My sister plays baseball.

3. The goldfish is in the bowl.

4. Have you seen my backpack?

Math

Look at the tally chart.
Then answer the questions.

Do you like scary stories?	
yes	卌 ||||
no	卌 卌 |||

5. Do more people like or dislike scary stories?   ○ like   ○ dislike

6. How many people like scary stories?   _____ people

Reading

Read. Then answer the item.

Leo knows it's winter when the air gets really cold. He puts on his winter coat to keep his body warm. He puts on his gloves to keep his hands warm. He puts on his hat to keep his head warm.

7. Draw lines to match.

cold body •   • wear hat

cold hands •   • wear gloves

cold head •   • wear coat

Language

Read the sentence. Circle the compound word.

1. I see a blue and yellow butterfly.

2. May I have some popcorn?

3. We grow vegetables in our backyard.

Math

Look at the tally chart.
Then answer the questions.

Have you ever petted a camel?	
yes	ⅧⅧ l
no	ⅧⅧⅧ llll

4. How many people have petted a camel? _____ people

5. How many people have not petted one? _____ people

Reading

Read. Then answer the item.

Pia gets eggs out of the henhouse before school. She likes telling the hens good morning as she puts each egg into the carton. Pia was always careful with the eggs, but one morning, the wind blew so hard that she dropped a few.

6. Underline the words that tell why Pia dropped the eggs.

Language

Match the words to make a compound word.
Then write the compound word you made.

1. camp •   • fish   _____

2. bed •   • fire   _____

3. jelly •   • cake   _____

4. cup •   • room   _____

Math

Look at the tally chart.
Then answer the questions.

How many did people see at the park?	
deer	卌 卌 卌 卌 卌 I
rabbits	卌 卌 I

5. What animal did people see more of?   _____

6. How many more?   ____ more

Reading

Read. Then answer the item.

Plants need heat and light to grow. When spring comes, plants get more heat and light. Some places get a lot of rain in spring. The rain helps plants grow, too.

7. Mark the things that help plants grow.

☐ heat   ☐ rain   ☐ spring   ☐ places

Language

Match the words to make a compound word.
Then write the compound word you made.

1. pan •   • ball   _____

2. rain •   • bow   _____

3. sea •   • cake   _____

4. foot •   • shell   _____

Math

Look at the tally chart.
Then answer the questions.

What do you usually have for breakfast?	
eggs	ＨＨＴ ＨＨＴ ＨＨＴ
cereal	ＨＨＴ ＨＨＴ ＨＨＴ ＨＨＴ
toast	ＨＨＴ ＨＨＴ

5. How many people told what they eat for breakfast?   _____ people

6. What do most people eat for breakfast?   _____

Reading

Read. Then answer the question.

Ming reads a book before bed each night. But sometimes she falls asleep before she finishes reading! When this happens, she wakes up an hour early the next morning. Then she feels tired all day at school.

7. What happens when Ming falls asleep too early?

_____

_____

Language

Use the word box to make compound words.

> tooth   bath   sun   corn
> tub   brush   pop   shine

1. _____

2. _____

3. _____

4. _____

Math

Read the word problem. Then answer the items.

In my class, 17 students have brown hair, 14 students have black hair, and 9 students have red hair.

Students' Hair Color	
brown	
black	
red	

5. Write tally marks in the chart to tell about the problem.

6. How many students are in the class altogether? _____ students

Reading

Read. Then answer the question.

Alex did not know why he kept losing things. He put a piece of candy in his pocket, but it was gone before he could eat it. He had also lost his good pen. It wasn't until his mom asked him how he got a hole in his pocket that Alex understood why he kept losing things.

7. What caused Alex to lose things?

_____

Language

Read the sentence. Then write **less** or **ful** to complete the sentence.

less   ful

1. The care_____ boy spilled milk on the floor.

2. The woman was always care_____ around fire.

Math

Look at the picture graph. Then answer the question.

☺ or ☹ = 1 student

Do you use an eraser cap on your pencil?	
☺ ☺ ☺ ☺ ☺	☹ ☹ ☹ ☹ ☹ ☹
yes	**no**

3. Do more students use eraser caps? Write **yes** or **no**. _____

Reading

Read. Then answer the items.

Sloth

This animal is called a **sloth**. It lives in trees in the jungle.

4. What does the title tell you?

_____

_____

5. Circle the sentences that tell you about the picture.

Daily Fundamentals • EMC 3241 • © Evan-Moor Corp.

Name ______________________________

Language

Read the sentence. Then write **re** or **un** to complete the sentence.

re   un

1. Paula was ______happy about her bad grade.

2. Please ______read the directions.

Math

Look at the picture graph. Then answer the question.

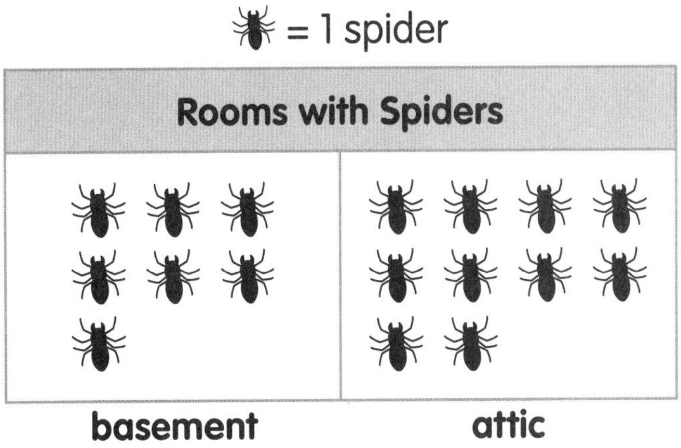

= 1 spider
Rooms with Spiders
basement
attic

3. Which room has more spiders? ______________

Reading

Read. Then answer the items.

Contents

What Pets Need.................... page 4
All About Dogs...................... page 10
All About Cats....................... page 16
All About Birds...................... page 22
All About Hamsters............. page 28
The Best Pet for You........... page 34

4. This contents page tells you ______.
   - ○ what is in the book and what page it's on
   - ○ who wrote the book and why it was written

5. What is this book about?

____

____

Language

Read the sentence. Then write **less** or **ful** to complete the sentence.

less   ful

1. Jose's painting was bright and color_____.

2. The fear_____ woman climbed the mountain.

Math

Look at the picture graph. Then answer the question.

☺ or ☹ = 1 person

Have you built a fort made of blankets?								
yes	☺	☺	☺	☺	☺	☺	☺	☺
no	☹	☹	☹					

3. How many people gave an answer altogether?   ____

Reading

Read. Then answer the questions.

ear tail eye leg nose foot mouth

4. What does this picture show you?

_____

_____

5. What do the words and lines tell you?

_____

_____

Language

Read the sentence. Then write **est** or **er** to complete the sentence.

> est   er

1. My teach_____ gave me homework.

2. I am the fast_____ runner at my school.

Math

Look at the picture graph. Then answer the question.

🍎 or 🍐 = 1 tree

Trees	
apple	🍎 🍎 🍎 🍎 🍎 🍎 🍎 🍎 🍎
pear	🍐 🍐 🍐 🍐

3. How many more apple trees are there than pear trees? _____

Reading

Look at the map. Then answer the item.

4. Mark the things the map shows.

   ☐ land

   ☐ water

   ☐ roads

   ☐ animals

   ☐ plants

   ☐ name of a country

Language

Read the sentence. Then write an affix to finish it.

less   ful   re   un

1. Kayla pushed the button

   to _____ start the game.

2. The table was spot_____ after Mom cleaned it.

3. Can you _____ do the lock?

Math

Read the word problem. Then answer the item.

Ethan found 6 colorful seashells and 4 white ones.

Seashells	
colorful	
white	

4. Finish the picture graph. Draw one 🐚 for each seashell.

Reading

Read. Then answer the items.

Evergreen Trees
Evergreen trees keep their leaves all year long. The leaves are strong, so they do not blow off.

5. Circle the headings.

6. What does a heading tell you?

   _____

   _____

Trees with Flat Leaves
Trees with flat leaves lose their leaves in the fall. The leaves dry up and fall off.

Language

Write the best word to finish the sentence. Then read the sentence.

1. I don't see _____ I know.
   anyone   **everyone**

2. I picked up _____ from the floor.
   anything   **everything**

Math

Look at the bar graph. Then answer the question.

Foods My Pet Snake Eats									
rodents									
lizards									
eggs									

1 2 3 4 5 6 7 8 9 10

3. What does the snake eat the most of?   _____

Reading

Read. Then answer the item.

Dogs are the best pets in the world! They never run away. They never make a mess. They always do what you tell them. Dogs have four legs. They also have tails.

4. Mark the sentence that tells what someone thinks or feels.

   ○ Dogs are the best pets in the world!

   ○ Dogs have four legs.

Language

Write the best word to finish the sentence. Then read the sentence.

1. Tristan likes _____ that has to do with video games.

   anyone   **anything**

2. Josie knows _____ in her class.

   everyone   **everything**

Math

Look at the bar graph. Then answer the questions.

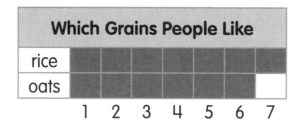

Which Grains People Like							
rice							
oats							

1 2 3 4 5 6 7

3. How many people like oats?   _____

4. Which grain do more people like?   _____

Reading

Read. Then answer the item.

My grandma was born in New York City in 1943. She has red hair and blue eyes. She is Irish. My grandma says that Irish people have the best parties. I hope that's true, because my birthday is next week!

5. Mark the sentence that tells a fact, or something that is true.

   ○ Irish people have the best parties.

   ○ My grandma was born in New York City in 1943.

Language

Write the best word to finish the sentence. Then read the sentence.

> everything   anything   everyone

1. Mom has _____ she needs to make a cake.

2. I cannot find _____ to wear.

Math

Look at the bar graph. Then answer the question.

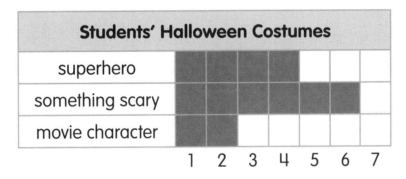

3. How many students altogether dressed in a costume? _____

Reading

Read. Then answer the item.

> A camel lives in a desert. A desert is hot and dry. There is not much food or water. A camel has fat in its hump. The fat helps the camel go without food for a long time. Camels are pretty animals.

4. Write one sentence that tells a fact about camels.

_____

_____

Language

Write the best word to finish the sentence. Then read the sentence.

> anyone   everyone   anything

1. Does _____ have their shoes on?

2. Has _____ seen my socks?

Math

Look at the bar graph. Then answer the questions.

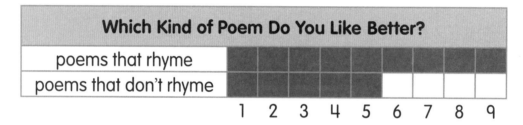

Which Kind of Poem Do You Like Better?								
poems that rhyme								
poems that don't rhyme								

1 2 3 4 5 6 7 8 9

3. How many more people like poems that rhyme? _____

4. How many answers are in the graph in all? _____

Reading

Read. Then answer the item.

I have the best bedroom in my house. My bed is soft and cozy. My red rug makes me feel happy. My two windows let in a lot of sunshine. My blue and yellow striped walls are fun to look at.

5. Write a sentence from the story that tells what someone thinks or feels.

_____

Language

Write the best word to finish the sentence. Then read the sentence.

> anyone   everyone   anything   everything

1. _____ in my family has black hair.

2. I don't think there is _____ left.

Math

Read the word problem. Then shade the graph to tell about the problem.

3. The bus stops at 4 schools, 7 gyms, and 9 parks.

Where the Bus Stops										
schools										
gyms										
parks										
	1	2	3	4	5	6	7	8	9	10

Reading

Read. Then answer the items.

Have you ever seen a ladybug in a garden? Ladybugs help plants stay healthy. They eat little bugs that hurt plants. One ladybug can eat 75 little bugs in one day. I like ladybugs.

4. Circle the sentence that tells what someone thinks or feels.

5. Draw a line under one sentence that tells a fact.

Language

Write the verb to tell what has **already happened**. Then read the sentence.

1. Sanji _____ me.
   help

2. Mr. Yin _____ dinner.
   cook

3. Don _____ loudly.
   talk

Math

Write **2-D** or **3-D** to tell about the shape.

4. _____

5. _____

6. _____

Reading

Read. Then answer the items.

Wesley was the first one in line to get a ball. He wrote his name on the list and picked a soccerball. He put his arms around the ball and held it tight to make sure no one could grab it from him.

7. What does the word **grab** mean?
   ○ ask   ○ take

8. What did Wesley do to make sure no one could grab the ball?

   _____

Language

Write the verb to tell what has **already happened**. Then read the sentence.

1. Sally _____ her foot.
   wash

2. Mary _____ her teeth.
   brush

3. Mike _____ Spanish.
   learn

Math

Draw a line. Match the object to the shape it looks like.

4. •   •

5. •   •

6. •   • (cube)

Reading

Read. Then answer the question.

My next door neighbor has a cat. It is always eating my cat's food. It comes to my back door and meows really loudly. One time it even ran into our house and ran after our cat. My next door neighbor's cat is such a pest.

7. Is being a **pest** a good thing or a bad thing? Tell how you know.

_____

_____

Language

Write the verb to tell what **will happen**. Then read the sentence.

1. Ken _____ his bed.
   make

2. Izzy _____ the bag.
   pack

3. Nell _____ a letter.
   write

Math

Draw a line. Match the object to the shape it looks like.

4.  •   •

5.  •   •

6.  •   •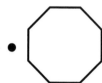

Reading

Read. Then answer the items.

Mr. Maris likes to walk around the neighborhood every morning. One rainy morning, he slipped, and his foot got stuck in a drain. "Help, I can't move!" yelled Mr. Maris. My family and I heard Mr. Maris yelling. My dad went outside to rescue him.

7. What does the word **rescue** mean?

   ○ help   ○ fix

8. What is another word you can use for **rescue**? _____

Language

Write the verb to tell what **will happen**. Then read the sentence.

1. Grandpa _____ the car. **start**

2. Mrs. Fields _____ the doctor. **call**

3. Ishmael _____ the sink. **fix**

Math

Mark the name of the shape.

4. ⬜
   ○ triangle
   ○ rectangle

5. ○
   ○ circle
   ○ square

6. △
   ○ cone
   ○ cube

Reading

Read. Then answer the items.

We have a lot of pets at my house. My mom and dad both love animals. My dad finds animals that need a home. The last time my dad brought home an animal, my mom had a big grin on her face. "Perfect!" she said. "I've always wanted a pet pig!"

7. Is a person with a **grin** happy or sad?

   ○ happy   ○ sad

8. What is another word you can use for **grin**? _____

Language

Read the sentence. Mark the circle that tells about it.

1. My brother will turn six this year.

   ○ already happened

   ○ will happen in the future

2. I looked for my hat everywhere.

   ○ already happened

   ○ will happen in the future

Math

Make a list. Write all the shapes you see in the snowman picture.

3.

_____

_____

_____

Reading

Read. Then answer the items.

My baby sister cries a lot. She cries really loudly when she is hungry. As soon as my mom gives her a bottle, she stops crying. Then the house is silent, and I can sleep.

4. What does the word **silent** mean? _____

5. Underline the words that help you know.

Daily Fundamentals • EMC 3241 • © Evan-Moor Corp.

Language

Write the best adjective to finish the sentence.

good   better   best

1. Those carrots taste _____.

2. The broccoli tastes _____ than the carrots.

3. The string beans taste the _____ of all.

Math

Look at the shape. Mark the answer to finish the sentence.

4.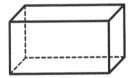

This shape _____.

○ has thickness

○ is flat

5.

This shape _____.

○ has thickness

○ is flat

Reading

Read. Then answer the items.

Nancy chopped carrots for the soup. Ben baked biscuits in the oven. Lynn set the table. When Mom and Dad got home, they said, "We love soup and biscuits! Thank you, kids!"

6. Where does this story happen?

_____

7. Draw a line under the words that help you know.

Language

Write the best adjective to finish the sentence.

bad   worse   worst

1. Lana's cold was _____ today.

2. It may get _____ tomorrow.

3. Thursday may be the _____ day of all.

Math

Look at the shape. Mark the answer to finish the sentence.

4.

This shape has _____.
- ○ 4 sides
- ○ 3 corners

5.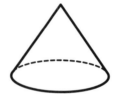

This shape has _____.
- ○ 1 curved surface
- ○ 2 corners

Reading

Read. Then answer the questions.

My mom loves sunflowers. Every spring, my dad plants sunflower seeds outside my mom's window. In the summer, they grow as tall as me! I love standing in the garden and pretending they are my friends.

6. Where does this story happen?

_____

7. Does this story happen at one time?   ○ yes   ○ no

Language

Write the best adjective to finish the sentence.

1. There was a _____ storm last night.

   bad   **worst**

2. All the rain will be _____ for the plants.

   better   **good**

Math

Look at the shape. Write the number of sides and corners.

3.

   _____ sides

   _____ corners

4.

   _____ sides

   _____ corners

5.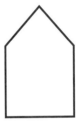

   _____ sides

   _____ corners

Reading

Read. Then answer the items.

The pet parade was only two days away, and everyone was talking about it! The store was crowded with people buying clothes for their pets. "I want my Snuggles to be pretty in pink," said Mrs. Rork as she paid for a tutu. "See you Saturday!" I said. I got to the parade early on Saturday. There were cats in tutus, dogs in cowboy hats, and pigs in clown costumes!

6. How much time passes in the story? _____

7. Draw a line under the words that help you know.

Language

Write the best adjective to finish the sentence.

1. This was the _____ birthday I ever had!

   best   better

2. Was it _____ than last year?

   best   better

Math

Look at the shape. Write the number of surfaces and corners.

3.

_____ surfaces

_____ corner

4.

_____ surfaces

_____ corners

5.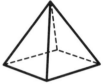

_____ surfaces

_____ corners

Reading

Read. Then answer the question.

Jeb lit a candle and got dressed. Pa had taken the wagon to sell the grain, so Jeb would have to walk a mile to the one-room schoolhouse. His teacher would have a fire lit to warm the room. Today was special, because a teacher from the next town was bringing an object called a globe. It would show them the world.

6. Is this story happening now or long ago? Tell how you know.

_____

Name _____

Language

Write the best adjective to finish the sentence.

good	better	best
bad	worse	worst

1. Jason is _____ at sports.

2. Nate is the _____ singer in our family.

3. Tasha has gotten _____ at cleaning up.

Math

Look at the shapes. Circle shapes that have curved surfaces. Draw a box around shapes that have flat surfaces. HINT: Some shapes have both.

4.

5.

6.

7.

8.

9.

Reading

Read. Then answer the question.

A sweet smell filled my nose. My eyes saw every color of the rainbow. Jelly beans, taffy, and lollipops as big as my head lined the walls. Kids jumped up and down as parents stood in line to pay for their treats. I looked around and wished I could buy everything.

10. Where does this story happen? Tell how you know.

_____

Language

Read the sentence. Write the correct word to finish the sentence.

1. May I have _____ chips?

   to   two

2. Raj went _____ school.
   to   two

3. My brother is _____ years old.   **to   two**

Math

Circle the two shapes that can be used to make the bigger shape.

4.

can make ⟶
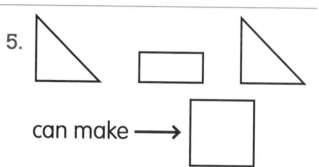

5.

can make ⟶

Reading

Read. Then answer the item.

The Sharks

This year my reading group is called The Sharks. We like to read about wild animals. We read about sharks, lions, and bears last week. This week, we will read about beavers, foxes, and zebras.

6. Mark the main idea with an **X**. Mark a detail with an **O**.

   ☐ The reading group likes to read about wild animals.

   ☐ This week, they will read about beavers, foxes, and zebras.

Language

Read the sentence. Write the correct word to finish the sentence.

1. I will be _____ soon.
   their   **there**

2. Is that _____ house?
   their   **there**

3. I've been _____ before.
   their   **there**

Math

Circle the two shapes that can be used to make the bigger shape.

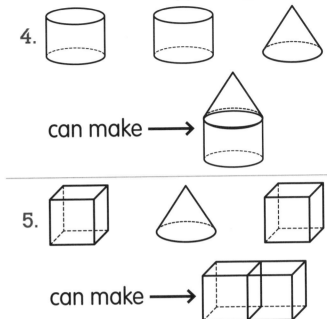

4.

can make ⟶

5.

can make ⟶

Reading

Read. Then answer the question.

Once upon a time, a small man lived in a small house. He only liked small things. One day, he went to buy a small bag of apples. He would use the apples to make a small pie. He opened his small gate and walked to town.

6. What is this story about?

_____

_____

Language

Read the sentence. Write the correct word to finish the sentence.

1. Do you _____ him?

   no   know

2. There is _____ more milk.

   no   know

3. I _____ you are right.

   no   know

Math

Draw a new shape using the two shapes given.

4.

5.

Reading

Read. Then answer the item.

My great grandpa says the world has changed a lot since he was a boy. Today, most families have cars. When he was a boy, only a few families had cars. He says that people sent each other letters in the mail. They did not have phones to call each other.

6. Mark the main idea with an **X**. Mark a detail with an **O**.

   ☐ When he was a boy, only a few families had cars.

   ☐ The world has changed a lot since my great grandpa was a boy.

Language

Read the sentence. Write the correct word to finish the sentence.

1. That is _____ cat's bowl.

   our   hour

2. We start school in one

   _____.

   our   hour

3. Let's have milk with

   _____ cookies.

   our   hour

Math

Draw a line from the group of shapes to the new shape you can make.

4.  •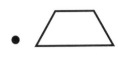

5. 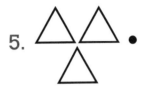 •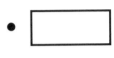

6.  •

Reading

Read. Then answer the items.

Many animals live in the Arctic. Polar bears call this cold, icy place home. Arctic foxes, walruses, and seals live in the Arctic, too. Some Arctic animals have thick fur to keep them warm. Some Arctic animals have white fur to help them hide in the snow.

7. Underline the main idea.

8. Write one detail.

_____

_____

Language

Read the sentence. Write the correct word to finish the sentence.

1. The bees are in _____ hive.

   their   **there**

2. The bear went _____ its cave.

   to   **two**

3. The forest is near _____ house.

   our   **hour**

Math

Draw a line from the group of shapes to the new shape you can make.

4. 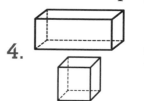 •   •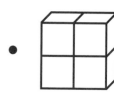

5. 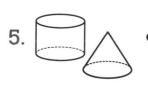 •   •

6. 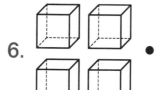 •   •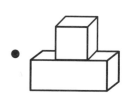

Reading

Read. Then answer the items.

My family likes to go to festivals. We eat foods from different countries. We went to the German festival last week and ate yummy baked breads. The week before that, we went to the Obon festival. The Greek festival is my favorite. I like to eat the Greek food and dance and yell, "Oompa!"

7. Underline the main idea.

8. Write one detail.

_____

_____

Language

Read the sentence. Write the meaning of the bold word.

1. Grandma used a brush to **scrub** the dirty carpet.

Scrub means _____.

to buy   to clean

Math

Look at the shape. Mark **equal** or **unequal** to tell about the shape's parts.

2.

   ○ equal
   ○ unequal

3.

   ○ equal
   ○ unequal

4.

   ○ equal
   ○ unequal

Reading

Read. Then answer the questions.

Kirk kicked his backpack all the way to the bus stop. He was so mad! His little sister had colored all over his math homework. Now he'd have to do it all again. He was glad that he had pulled one of her curls and made her cry.

5. How do you think Kirk is feeling?

_____

6. How is Kirk acting? _____

Language

Read the sentence. Write the meaning of the bold word.

1. The sleepy parents **awoke** when the baby cried.

   Awoke means _____.

                woke up   **ran**

Math

Look at the shape. Mark **equal** or **unequal** to tell about the shape's parts.

2.

   ○ equal
   ○ unequal

3.

   ○ equal
   ○ unequal

4.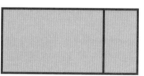

   ○ equal
   ○ unequal

Reading

Read. Then answer the items.

    The man who works at the corner store is really tall. He has brown skin and big brown eyes. He also has a big smile. Most days he wears loose white clothes and brown sandals. He does not speak much English, but he always waves and says, "Good day!" when I leave.

5. Draw a line under the words that tell you what the man looks like.

6. How does the man act? _____

Language

Read the sentence. Write the meaning of the bold word.

1. Lincoln School puts on a Christmas **play** every year.

   In this sentence, **play** means _____.

   to have fun   a story acted out

Math

Circle the shape if it has equal parts.

2.

4.

6.

3.

5.

7.

Reading

Read. Then answer the question.

Mr. Suro teaches science every Friday. He always brings something for us to see and touch. He likes for us to ask him questions. He says he's here to help us learn. Today, he told us that water, tree roots, and animals can make rocks break apart. Then he let us feel the cracked rocks he brought.

8. Would you want to be in Mr. Suro's class? Tell why or why not.

_____

Language

Read the sentence. Write the meaning of the bold word.

1. A black **fly** landed on my dinner plate.

   In this sentence, **fly** means _____.

   an insect   **to move through the air**

Math

Circle the shape if it has equal parts.

2.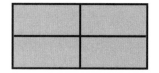

4.

6.

3.

5.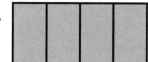

7.

Reading

Read. Then answer the question.

Jason wanted to be the first in line, so he jumped out of his seat and ran to the door as soon as the bell rang. On his way, he stepped on Nicole's toe and knocked over Daniel's books. "Ouch!" said Nicole. "Hey!" said Daniel. Jason felt bad about what happened. "Sorry, I should not have run. Are you guys okay?" asked Jason.

8. What lesson did Jason learn? _____

Language

Read the sentence. Write the meaning of the bold word.

1. The baseball player has a strong **bat**.

   In this sentence, **bat** means _____.

   an animal   **an object used to hit**

Math

Draw a line on the shape to give it two equal parts.

2.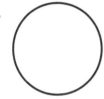

3.

4.

Reading

Read. Then answer the item.

Blanca told her sister not to be scared as she hugged her. Blanca moved slowly and quietly toward the big black spider on the wall. When she got close, she put a cup over the spider and quietly carried it outside. "Thank you!" said Blanca's sister. "No problem," said Blanca.

5. Write a sentence that tells about how Blanca acts.

_____

Language

Read the paragraph. Think about what the bold word means.

The cafeteria is **huge**! All 500 students can eat lunch in it at the same time.

1. Write a sentence about a place you've been that is **huge**.

_____

_____

Math

Mark **halves** or **fourths** to tell about the shape's parts.

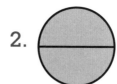

2. ○ halves
    ○ fourths

3. ○ halves
    ○ fourths

4. ○ halves
    ○ fourths

Reading

Read. Then answer the items.

Chocolate is yummy! I like chocolate because it tastes sweet, and it melts in my mouth.

5. Mark the word that tells about the text.

   ○ fact   ○ opinion

In 1903, Milton Hershey built the first modern chocolate factory. Then he built a town around it called Hershey, Pennsylvania.

6. Mark the word that tells about the text.

   ○ fact   ○ opinion

Daily Fundamentals • EMC 3241 • © Evan-Moor Corp.

Name _____

Language

Read the paragraph. Think about what the bold word means.

My sister is **kind**. She helps me with my chores. She lets me share her snack and play with her toys.

1. Write a sentence about a person who is **kind**.

_____

_____

Math

Circle the shape in the pair that shows halves.

2.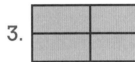

3.

4.

Reading

Read. Then answer the items.

France gave America a gift in 1886. France is a nice country. The gift was a statue that is a symbol of America's freedom. It is called the Statue of Liberty. It is a very tall statue. There are 354 steps inside of it. It is a really beautiful gift.

5. Write one fact from the text.

_____

_____

6. Draw a line under one sentence that gives an opinion.

Language

Read the paragraph. Think about what the bold word means.

> The school bus is **crowded**. Kids fill every seat. They can hardly fit their backpacks.

1. Write a sentence about a place you've been that is **crowded**.

_____

_____

Math

Circle the shape in the pair that shows fourths.

2.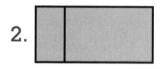

3.

4.

Reading

Read. Then answer the item.

> The state of Idaho grows a lot of potatoes. It has just the right kind of soil. There is snow in the winter. When the snow melts, the cool water helps the potato plants grow. Potatoes are used to make chips and french fries.

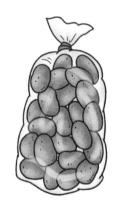

5. Write one fact from the text.

_____

_____

Language

Read the paragraph. Think about what the bold word means.

"Don't cut your hand," warned Grandma. "The roses are pretty, but the thorns are **sharp**!" she said.

1. Write a sentence about something **sharp**.

   _____

   _____

Math

Write **whole**, **half**, or **fourth** to tell about the shaded part of the shape.

2. 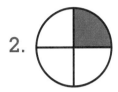 _____

3.  _____

4.  _____

Reading

Read. Then answer the items.

Most of the kids in my class play a sport after school. Sixteen kids play soccer, and seven play baseball. Only two of us play football. I think everyone should play football because it is the best sport.

5. Draw a line under the sentence that gives an opinion.

6. Write a sentence that gives an opinion about baseball.

   _____

   _____

Language

Read the paragraph. Think about what the bold word means.

Our new puppy is really **shy**. It hides under the chair and watches Mom and Dad. It will only come out to see me.

1. Write a sentence about someone who is **shy**.

_____

_____

Math

Draw a line or lines on the shape to show halves or fourths.

2. Give the shape halves.

3. Give the shape fourths.

Reading

Read. Then answer the items.

Theodor Seuss Geisel was born in 1904. He loved to draw, and he loved to go to the zoo. Theodor became "Dr. Seuss" when he started writing books for children. He wrote *The Cat in the Hat*. He also wrote *Green Eggs and Ham*.

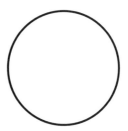
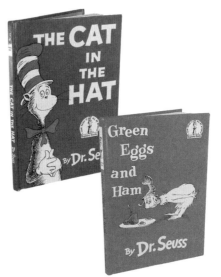

Julie Clopper / Shutterstock.com

4. Write a fact about Dr. Seuss.

_____

5. Write your opinion about Dr. Seuss books.

_____

Answer Key

Page 11

Name _____

Day 1 | Week 1

Language

Mark the circle that names a **person**.

1. ○ sit ● boy
2. ● mom ○ see
3. ○ run ● man

Math

Count how many. Write the number.

4. _4_ frogs

5. _7_ butterflies

Reading

Read. Then answer the question.

Pat has a cat. Pat has a rat.
Her cat is on a mat. Her rat has a hat.

6. Who is this story about?
   ● Pat and her pets
   ○ a mat and a hat

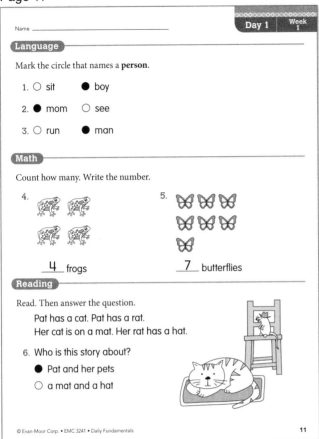

© Evan-Moor Corp. • EMC 3241 • Daily Fundamentals   11

Page 12

Name _____

Day 2 | Week 1

Language

Mark the circle that names a **place**.

1. ● park ○ play
2. ○ help ● school
3. ○ get ● home

Math

Count how many in each group. Circle the group that has 8.

4.

Reading

Read. Then answer the question.

What did I do today?
I had fun.
I ate a hot dog on a bun.
I sat in the sun.

5. What is this story about?
   ○ a sunny day
   ● a boy who had fun

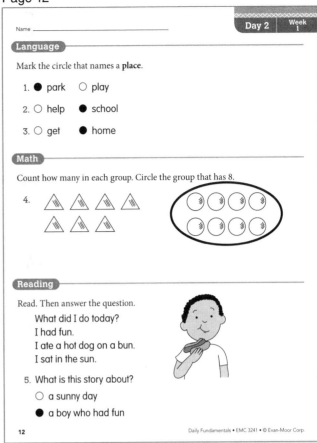

12   Daily Fundamentals • EMC 3241 • © Evan-Moor Corp.

Page 13

Name _____

Day 3 | Week 1

Language

Mark the circle that names a **thing**.

1. ○ like ● book
2. ● hat ○ cook
3. ○ sat ● fan

Math

Count how many. Write the number.

4. _10_ dots

5. _6_ dots

Reading

Read. Then answer the question.

Mom can mop. I can hop.
Tim can pop. Dad can chop.
We can not stop.
We can mop, hop, pop, and chop!

6. What is this story about?
   ○ where people can go
   ● what people can do

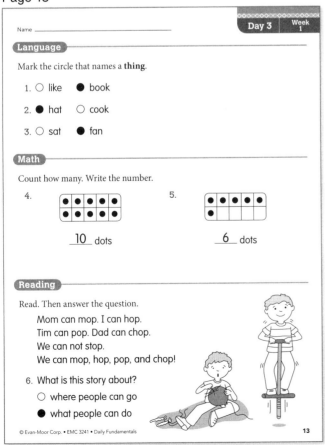

© Evan-Moor Corp. • EMC 3241 • Daily Fundamentals   13

Page 14

Name _____

Day 4 | Week 1

Language

Mark the circle that names an **animal**.

1. ● pig ○ wig
2. ○ mat ● cat
3. ● bug ○ rug

Math

Count to 15. Then draw 15 dots in the box.

4.

Reading

Read. Then answer the question.

I see a bug on a rug. Come here, bug!
Now the bug is on the mug. Come here, bug!
Now the bug is on me.
I will give the bug a hug.

5. What is this story about?
   ● a boy and a bug
   ○ a rug and a mug

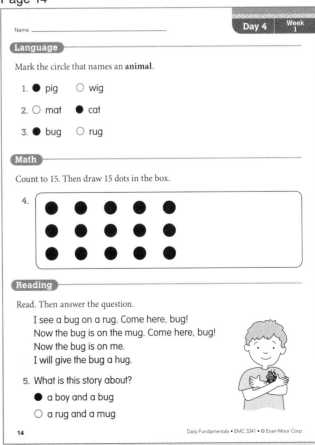

14   Daily Fundamentals • EMC 3241 • © Evan-Moor Corp.

Page 15

Name _____

Day 5 | Week 1

Language

A noun is a person, place, animal, or thing. Circle the noun.

1. The (girl) hops.
2. The (man) sits.
3. This is the (park).

Math

Count to 20. Write the numbers on the lines.

4. 1 2 3 4 5 6 7
   8 9 10 11 12 13 14
   15 16 17 18 19 20

Reading

Read. Then answer the question.

My name is Jill. I am going to a farm.
I want to see where sheep live.
I want to see sheep eat.
I want to pet sheep.

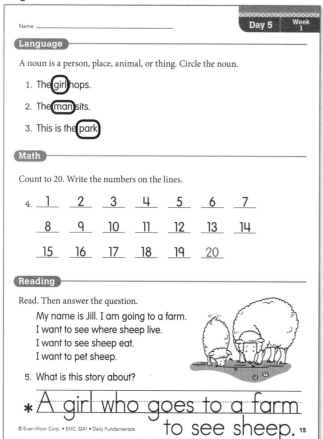

5. What is this story about?

* A girl who goes to a farm to see sheep.

© Evan-Moor Corp. • EMC 3241 • Daily Fundamentals   15

Page 16

Name _____

Day 1 | Week 2

Language

Circle the word that tells what the boy is doing.

1. The boy (jumps)
2. The boy (eats)
3. The boy (sleeps)

Math

Read the problem. Count on to answer the question.

4. There are 17 eggs in the basket. How many eggs are there in all?

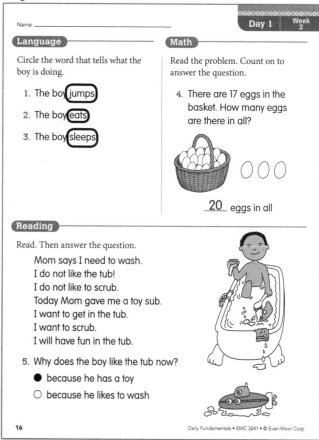

___20___ eggs in all

Reading

Read. Then answer the question.

Mom says I need to wash.
I do not like the tub!
I do not like to scrub.
Today Mom gave me a toy sub.
I want to get in the tub.
I want to scrub.
I will have fun in the tub.

5. Why does the boy like the tub now?
   ● because he has a toy
   ○ because he likes to wash

16   Daily Fundamentals • EMC 3241 • © Evan-Moor Corp.

Page 17

Name _____

Day 2 | Week 2

Language

What do the kids **do**? Mark the circle.

1. The kids walk home.
   ○ home   ● walk
2. The kids eat food.
   ● eat   ○ food
3. The kids play ball.
   ● play   ○ ball

Math

Count on. Write all the numbers. Then write how many in all.

4. ♥♥♥♥♥♥♥♥♥
   ♥♥♥♥♥♥♥♥♥
   18

   ♥   ♥   ♥
   19   20   21

   ___21___ hearts in all

Reading

Read. Then answer the question.

What is in the pot?
It is not cold. It is hot.
It smells good.
It will hit the spot!

5. What do you think is in the pot?

* I think soup or another food is in the pot.

© Evan-Moor Corp. • EMC 3241 • Daily Fundamentals   17

Page 18

Name _____

Day 3 | Week 2

Language

What do the people **do**? Mark the circle.

1. Dad makes cake.
   ● makes   ○ cake
2. Mom cooks ham.
   ○ ham   ● cooks
3. Liz plays ball.
   ● plays   ○ ball

Math

Count on. Write how many.

4.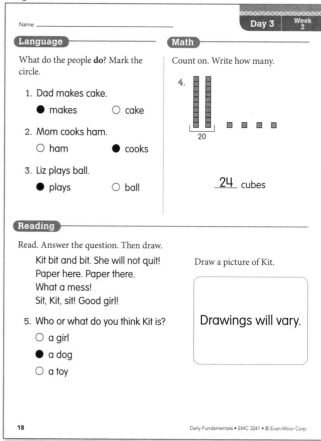
   20

   ___24___ cubes

Reading

Read. Answer the question. Then draw.

Kit bit and bit. She will not quit!
Paper here. Paper there.
What a mess!
Sit, Kit, sit! Good girl!

Draw a picture of Kit.

┌─────────────────┐
│   │
│ Drawings will vary. │
│   │
└─────────────────┘

5. Who or what do you think Kit is?
   ○ a girl
   ● a dog
   ○ a toy

18   Daily Fundamentals • EMC 3241 • © Evan-Moor Corp.

Page 19

Name _____

Day 4 | Week 2

Language

Circle the action word.

1. Tran (reads) his book.
2. Kim (pets) the dog.
3. Jeff (rides) his bike.

Math

Use the number line to count on. Write the numbers.

4.
24 __25__ 26 __27__ 28

5.
26 __27__ __28__ __29__ 30

Reading

Read the story. Then answer the question.

Goodbye summer.
I know it is fall.
The wind is here.
The wind is here every day.

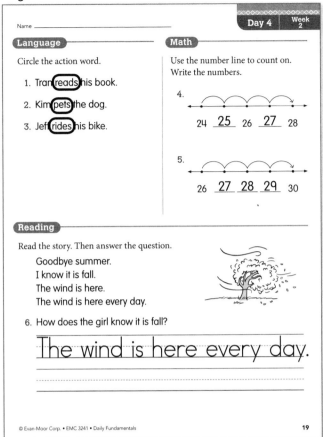

6. How does the girl know it is fall?

__The wind is here every day.__

Page 20

Name _____

Day 5 | Week 2

Language

Finish the sentence. Write an action word.

[hops   sits]

1. The bunny __hops__ .

2. The man __sits__ .

Math

Count on to finish the chart. Write the numbers.

3.

25	26	27	28
29	30	31	32
33	34	35	36
37	38	39	40

Reading

Read. Then answer the question.

There was a bird that had a nest.
The nest was in an apple tree.
A cat looked at the bird.
Then up and up went the cat.
Then down and down went the cat.
Where was that bird?

4. What do you think happened?

★ __I think the cat got the bird.__
__I think the bird flew away.__

Page 21

Name _____

Day 1 | Week 3

Language

Circle the word that tells about **size**.

1. My dad is (tall).
2. My sister is (small).
3. My pet is (big).

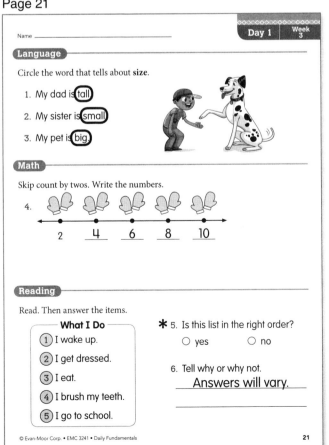

Math

Skip count by twos. Write the numbers.

4.
2 __4__ __6__ __8__ __10__

Reading

Read. Then answer the items.

What I Do
1. I wake up.
2. I get dressed.
3. I eat.
4. I brush my teeth.
5. I go to school.

★ 5. Is this list in the right order?
   ○ yes   ○ no

6. Tell why or why not.
   __Answers will vary.__

Page 22

Name _____

Day 2 | Week 3

Language

Circle the word that tells **how many**.

1. I see (two) bikes.
2. I want (one) bike.
3. I will ride it (five) times.

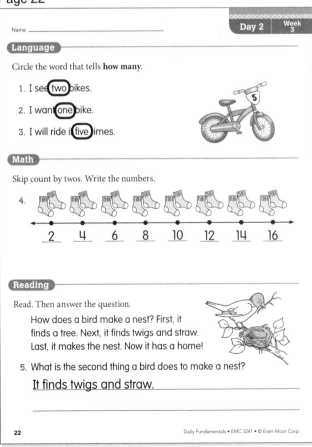

Math

Skip count by twos. Write the numbers.

4.
__2__ __4__ __6__ __8__ __10__ __12__ __14__ __16__

Reading

Read. Then answer the question.

How does a bird make a nest? First, it finds a tree. Next, it finds twigs and straw. Last, it makes the nest. Now it has a home!

5. What is the second thing a bird does to make a nest?
   __It finds twigs and straw.__

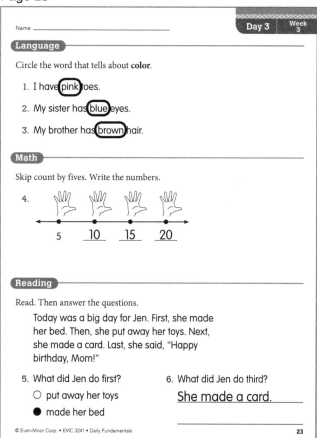

✱ These answers will vary. Examples are given.

Page 23

Name _____

Day 3 | Week 3

Language

Circle the word that tells about **color**.

1. I have (pink) toes.
2. My sister has (blue) eyes.
3. My brother has (brown) hair.

Math

Skip count by fives. Write the numbers.

4.

5   10   15   20

Reading

Read. Then answer the questions.

Today was a big day for Jen. First, she made her bed. Then, she put away her toys. Next, she made a card. Last, she said, "Happy birthday, Mom!"

5. What did Jen do first?
   ○ put away her toys
   ● made her bed

6. What did Jen do third?

   She made a card.

© Evan-Moor Corp. • EMC 3241 • Daily Fundamentals   23

Page 24

Name _____

Day 4 | Week 3

Language

Which word tells how something **feels**?

1. The water is warm.   ○ water   ● warm
2. The grass feels wet.   ● wet   ○ the
3. The cat's fur is soft.   ○ cat's   ● soft

Math

Skip count by fives. Write the numbers.

4.

5   10   15   20   25   30

Reading

Read. Then write **1, 2, 3, 4** to tell what happened.

Dad fills a tub with water. Spot jumps in the tub. Dad scrubs Spot. Spot jumps out of the tub.

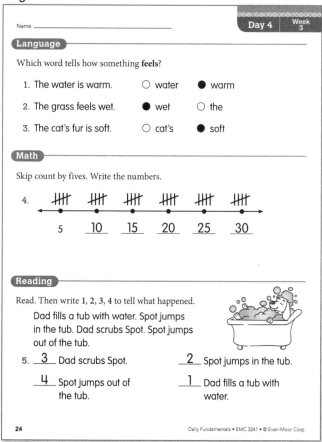

5. _3_ Dad scrubs Spot.   _2_ Spot jumps in the tub.

   _4_ Spot jumps out of the tub.   _1_ Dad fills a tub with water.

24   Daily Fundamentals • EMC 3241 • © Evan-Moor Corp.

Page 25

Name _____

Day 5 | Week 3

Language

Write the word that tells about the dog.

1. It is a small dog.   small
2. The dog is brown.   brown
3. The dog is furry.   furry

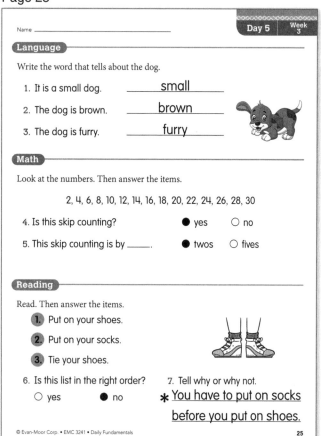

Math

Look at the numbers. Then answer the items.

2, 4, 6, 8, 10, 12, 14, 16, 18, 20, 22, 24, 26, 28, 30

4. Is this skip counting?   ● yes   ○ no
5. This skip counting is by _____.   ● twos   ○ fives

Reading

Read. Then answer the items.

1. Put on your shoes.
2. Put on your socks.
3. Tie your shoes.

6. Is this list in the right order?
   ○ yes   ● no

7. Tell why or why not.

   ✱ You have to put on socks before you put on shoes.

© Evan-Moor Corp. • EMC 3241 • Daily Fundamentals   25

Page 26

Name _____

Day 1 | Week 4

Language

Circle the word that names **more than one**.

1. (girls)   girl
2. (balls)   ball
3. hat   (hats)

Math

Read the problem. Count on to answer the question.

4. There are 28 cookies in the jar. How many cookies are there in all?

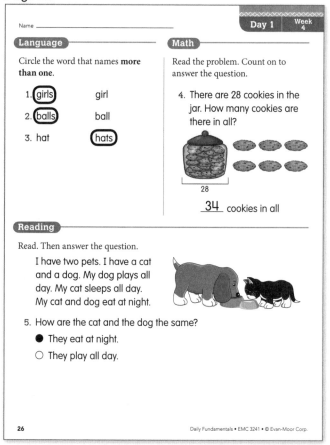

28

_34_ cookies in all

Reading

Read. Then answer the question.

I have two pets. I have a cat and a dog. My dog plays all day. My cat sleeps all day. My cat and dog eat at night.

5. How are the cat and the dog the same?
   ● They eat at night.
   ○ They play all day.

26   Daily Fundamentals • EMC 3241 • © Evan-Moor Corp.

Page 27

Name _____

Day 2 | Week 4

Language

Circle the word that names **more than one**.

1. hand — (hands)
2. (apples) — apple
3. cow — (cows)

Math

Count on. Write all the numbers. Then write how many in all.

4.

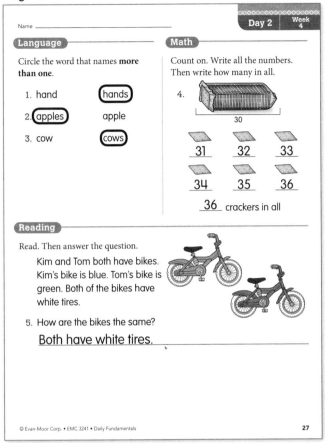

30

31 32 33
34 35 36

__36__ crackers in all

Reading

Read. Then answer the question.

Kim and Tom both have bikes. Kim's bike is blue. Tom's bike is green. Both of the bikes have white tires.

5. How are the bikes the same?

__Both have white tires.__

© Evan-Moor Corp. • EMC 3241 • Daily Fundamentals   27

Page 28

Name _____

Day 3 | Week 4

Language

Write **s** to make a word that names **more than one**.

1. The boy__s__ play.
2. The owl__s__ hoot.
3. The bat__s__ fly.

Math

Count on. Write how many.

4.

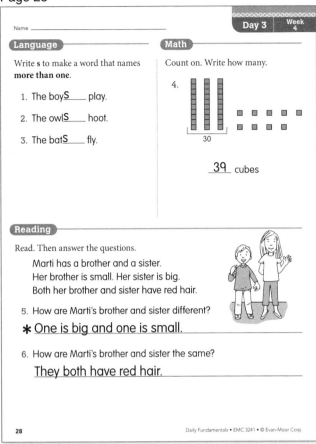

30

__39__ cubes

Reading

Read. Then answer the questions.

Marti has a brother and a sister. Her brother is small. Her sister is big. Both her brother and sister have red hair.

5. How are Marti's brother and sister different?

∗ __One is big and one is small.__

6. How are Marti's brother and sister the same?

__They both have red hair.__

28   Daily Fundamentals • EMC 3241 • © Evan-Moor Corp.

Page 29

Name _____

Day 4 | Week 4

Language

Write **es** to make a word that names **more than one**.

1. I see the box__es__ .
2. I like dress__es__ .
3. I make wish__es__ .

Math

Use the number line to count on.

4.

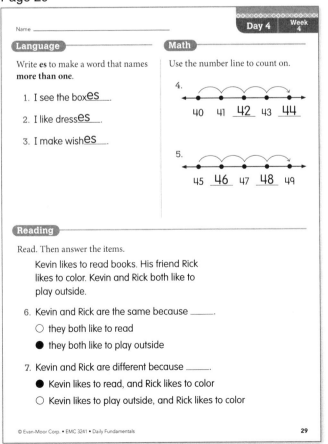

40 41 __42__ 43 __44__

5.

45 __46__ 47 __48__ 49

Reading

Read. Then answer the items.

Kevin likes to read books. His friend Rick likes to color. Kevin and Rick both like to play outside.

6. Kevin and Rick are the same because ____.
   ○ they both like to read
   ● they both like to play outside

7. Kevin and Rick are different because ____.
   ● Kevin likes to read, and Rick likes to color
   ○ Kevin likes to play outside, and Rick likes to color

© Evan-Moor Corp. • EMC 3241 • Daily Fundamentals   29

Page 30

Name _____

Day 5 | Week 4

Language

Circle the word that goes with the picture.

1. box — (boxes)
2. (rats) — rat
3. (bird) — birds

Math

Count on to finish the chart. Write the numbers.

4.

45	46	47	48
49	50	51	52
53	54	55	56
57	58	59	60

Reading

Read. Then answer the questions.

Many animals live in ponds. Frogs live in ponds. Frogs hop to the pond. Ducks live in ponds. Ducks fly to the pond. Both frogs and ducks like water.

5. What is the same about frogs and ducks?

∗ __Frogs and ducks live in ponds.__

6. What is different about frogs and ducks?

∗ __Frogs hop and ducks fly.__

30   Daily Fundamentals • EMC 3241 • © Evan-Moor Corp.

Page 31

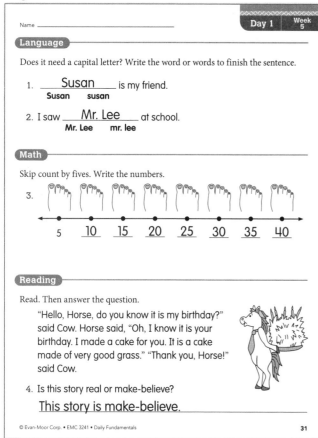

Name _____

Day 1 | Week 5

Language

Does it need a capital letter? Write the word or words to finish the sentence.

1. ___Susan___ is my friend.
   Susan   susan

2. I saw ___Mr. Lee___ at school.
   Mr. Lee   mr. lee

Math

Skip count by fives. Write the numbers.

3.

5 _10_ _15_ _20_ _25_ _30_ _35_ _40_

Reading

Read. Then answer the question.

"Hello, Horse, do you know it is my birthday?" said Cow. Horse said, "Oh, I know it is your birthday. I made a cake for you. It is a cake made of very good grass." "Thank you, Horse!" said Cow.

4. Is this story real or make-believe?

   This story is make-believe.

© Evan-Moor Corp. • EMC 3241 • Daily Fundamentals   31

Page 32

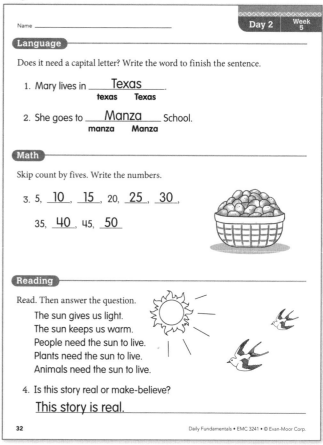

Name _____

Day 2 | Week 5

Language

Does it need a capital letter? Write the word to finish the sentence.

1. Mary lives in ___Texas___.
   texas   **Texas**

2. She goes to ___Manza___ School.
   manza   **Manza**

Math

Skip count by fives. Write the numbers.

3. 5, _10_, _15_, 20, _25_, _30_, 35, _40_, 45, _50_

Reading

Read. Then answer the question.

The sun gives us light.
The sun keeps us warm.
People need the sun to live.
Plants need the sun to live.
Animals need the sun to live.

4. Is this story real or make-believe?

   This story is real.

32   Daily Fundamentals • EMC 3241 • © Evan-Moor Corp.

Page 33

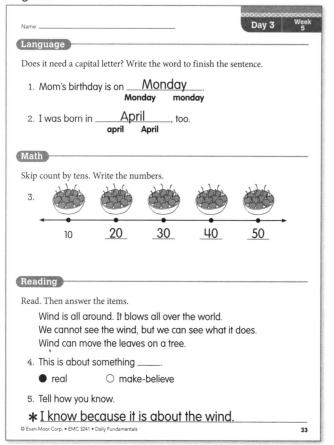

Name _____

Day 3 | Week 5

Language

Does it need a capital letter? Write the word to finish the sentence.

1. Mom's birthday is on ___Monday___.
   Monday   monday

2. I was born in ___April___, too.
   april   **April**

Math

Skip count by tens. Write the numbers.

3.

10 _20_ _30_ _40_ _50_

Reading

Read. Then answer the items.

Wind is all around. It blows all over the world.
We cannot see the wind, but we can see what it does.
Wind can move the leaves on a tree.

4. This is about something ___.
   ● real   ○ make-believe

5. Tell how you know.

   ✱I know because it is about the wind.

© Evan-Moor Corp. • EMC 3241 • Daily Fundamentals   33

Page 34

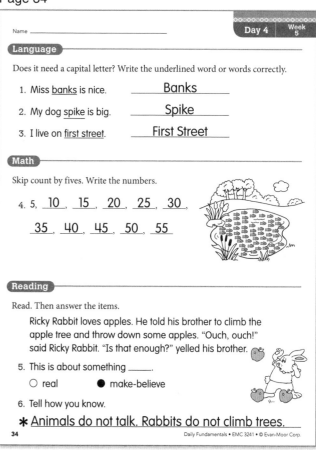

Name _____

Day 4 | Week 5

Language

Does it need a capital letter? Write the underlined word or words correctly.

1. Miss banks is nice.   ___Banks___

2. My dog spike is big.   ___Spike___

3. I live on first street.   ___First Street___

Math

Skip count by fives. Write the numbers.

4. 5, _10_, _15_, _20_, _25_, _30_, _35_, _40_, _45_, _50_, _55_

Reading

Read. Then answer the items.

Ricky Rabbit loves apples. He told his brother to climb the apple tree and throw down some apples. "Ouch, ouch!" said Ricky Rabbit. "Is that enough?" yelled his brother.

5. This is about something ___.
   ○ real   ● make-believe

6. Tell how you know.

   ✱Animals do not talk. Rabbits do not climb trees.

34   Daily Fundamentals • EMC 3241 • © Evan-Moor Corp.

✱ These answers will vary. Examples are given.

Page 35

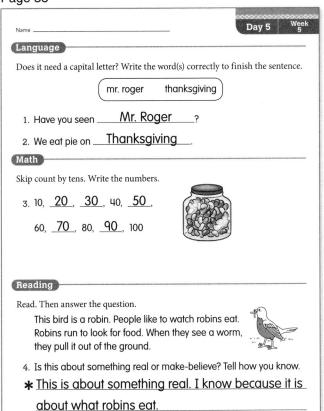

Name _____

Day 5 | Week 5

Language

Does it need a capital letter? Write the word(s) correctly to finish the sentence.

| mr. roger   thanksgiving |

1. Have you seen ___Mr. Roger___ ?

2. We eat pie on ___Thanksgiving___ .

Math

Skip count by tens. Write the numbers.

3. 10, __20__, __30__, 40, __50__,

60, __70__, 80, __90__, 100

Reading

Read. Then answer the question.

This bird is a robin. People like to watch robins eat. Robins run to look for food. When they see a worm, they pull it out of the ground.

4. Is this about something real or make-believe? Tell how you know.

✱ This is about something real. I know because it is about what robins eat.

Page 36

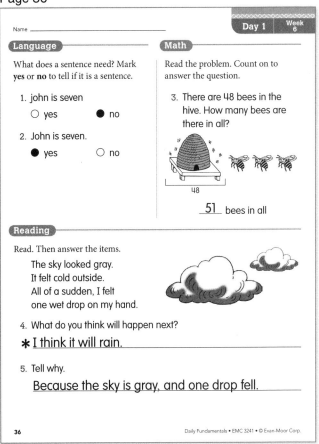

Name _____

Day 1 | Week 6

Language

What does a sentence need? Mark **yes** or **no** to tell if it is a sentence.

1. john is seven
   ○ yes ● no

2. John is seven.
   ● yes ○ no

Math

Read the problem. Count on to answer the question.

3. There are 48 bees in the hive. How many bees are there in all?

48

__51__ bees in all

Reading

Read. Then answer the items.

The sky looked gray.
It felt cold outside.
All of a sudden, I felt
one wet drop on my hand.

4. What do you think will happen next?

✱ I think it will rain.

5. Tell why.

Because the sky is gray, and one drop fell.

Page 37

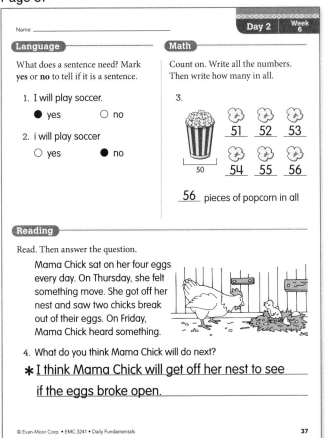

Name _____

Day 2 | Week 6

Language

What does a sentence need? Mark **yes** or **no** to tell if it is a sentence.

1. I will play soccer.
   ● yes ○ no

2. i will play soccer
   ○ yes ● no

Math

Count on. Write all the numbers. Then write how many in all.

3.

50

__51__ __52__ __53__
__54__ __55__ __56__

__56__ pieces of popcorn in all

Reading

Read. Then answer the question.

Mama Chick sat on her four eggs every day. On Thursday, she felt something move. She got off her nest and saw two chicks break out of their eggs. On Friday, Mama Chick heard something.

4. What do you think Mama Chick will do next?

✱ I think Mama Chick will get off her nest to see if the eggs broke open.

Page 38

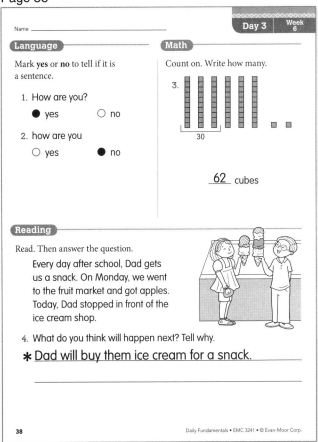

Name _____

Day 3 | Week 6

Language

Mark **yes** or **no** to tell if it is a sentence.

1. How are you?
   ● yes ○ no

2. how are you
   ○ yes ● no

Math

Count on. Write how many.

3.

30

__62__ cubes

Reading

Read. Then answer the question.

Every day after school, Dad gets us a snack. On Monday, we went to the fruit market and got apples. Today, Dad stopped in front of the ice cream shop.

4. What do you think will happen next? Tell why.

✱ Dad will buy them ice cream for a snack.

Page 39

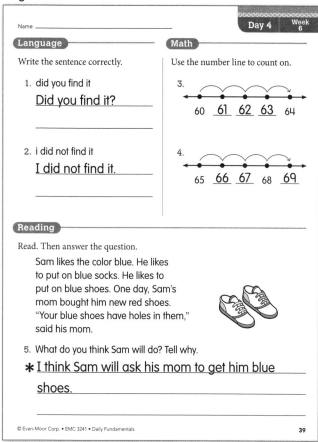

Name _____

Day 4 | **Week 6**

Language

Write the sentence correctly.

1. did you find it

   <u>Did you find it?</u>

2. i did not find it

   <u>I did not find it.</u>

Math

Use the number line to count on.

3. 60 <u>61 62 63</u> 64

4. 65 <u>66 67</u> 68 <u>69</u>

Reading

Read. Then answer the question.

Sam likes the color blue. He likes to put on blue socks. He likes to put on blue shoes. One day, Sam's mom bought him new red shoes. "Your blue shoes have holes in them," said his mom.

5. What do you think Sam will do? Tell why.

* <u>I think Sam will ask his mom to get him blue</u>
<u>shoes.</u>

© Evan-Moor Corp. • EMC 3241 • Daily Fundamentals   39

Page 40

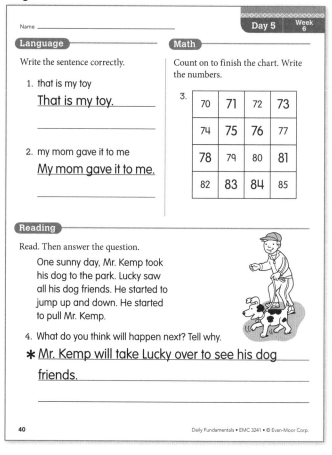

Name _____

Day 5 | **Week 6**

Language

Write the sentence correctly.

1. that is my toy

   <u>That is my toy.</u>

2. my mom gave it to me

   <u>My mom gave it to me.</u>

Math

Count on to finish the chart. Write the numbers.

3.

70	71	72	73
74	75	76	77
78	79	80	81
82	83	84	85

Reading

Read. Then answer the question.

One sunny day, Mr. Kemp took his dog to the park. Lucky saw all his dog friends. He started to jump up and down. He started to pull Mr. Kemp.

4. What do you think will happen next? Tell why.

* <u>Mr. Kemp will take Lucky over to see his dog</u>
<u>friends.</u>

40   Daily Fundamentals • EMC 3241 • © Evan-Moor Corp.

Page 41

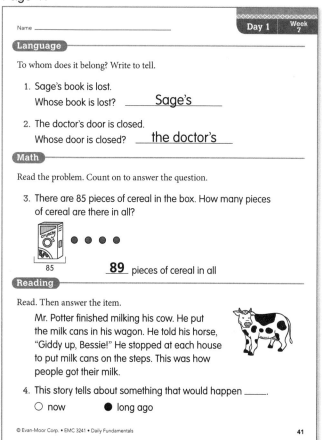

Name _____

Day 1 | **Week 7**

Language

To whom does it belong? Write to tell.

1. Sage's book is lost.
   Whose book is lost?   <u>Sage's</u>

2. The doctor's door is closed.
   Whose door is closed?   <u>the doctor's</u>

Math

Read the problem. Count on to answer the question.

3. There are 85 pieces of cereal in the box. How many pieces of cereal are there in all?

   85 • • • •

   <u>89</u> pieces of cereal in all

Reading

Read. Then answer the item.

Mr. Potter finished milking his cow. He put the milk cans in his wagon. He told his horse, "Giddy up, Bessie!" He stopped at each house to put milk cans on the steps. This was how people got their milk.

4. This story tells about something that would happen _____.

   ○ now   ● long ago

© Evan-Moor Corp. • EMC 3241 • Daily Fundamentals   41

Page 42

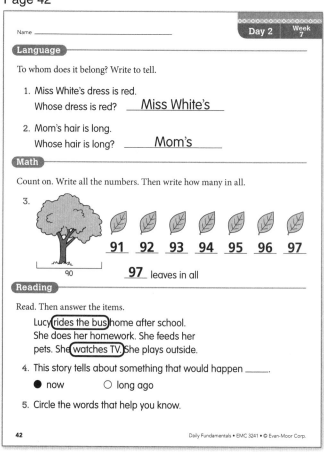

Name _____

Day 2 | **Week 7**

Language

To whom does it belong? Write to tell.

1. Miss White's dress is red.
   Whose dress is red?   <u>Miss White's</u>

2. Mom's hair is long.
   Whose hair is long?   <u>Mom's</u>

Math

Count on. Write all the numbers. Then write how many in all.

3.

   90 <u>91</u> <u>92</u> <u>93</u> <u>94</u> <u>95</u> <u>96</u> <u>97</u>

   <u>97</u> leaves in all

Reading

Read. Then answer the items.

Lucy (rides the bus) home after school. She does her homework. She feeds her pets. She (watches TV.) She plays outside.

4. This story tells about something that would happen _____.

   ● now   ○ long ago

5. Circle the words that help you know.

42   Daily Fundamentals • EMC 3241 • © Evan-Moor Corp.

Page 43

Language

Write 's to show to whom it belongs.

1. My sister__'s__ cat is named Fluffy.
2. Fluffy__'s__ fur is soft and white.
3. My cat__'s__ name is Stripes.

Math

Count on. Write how many.

4.

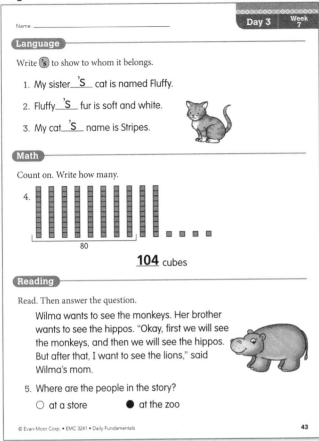

80

104 cubes

Reading

Read. Then answer the question.

Wilma wants to see the monkeys. Her brother wants to see the hippos. "Okay, first we will see the monkeys, and then we will see the hippos. But after that, I want to see the lions," said Wilma's mom.

5. Where are the people in the story?
   ○ at a store   ● at the zoo

Page 44

Language

Write 's to show to whom or to what it belongs.

1. The man__'s__ hands are big.
2. Kaleb__'s__ tooth is loose.
3. The horse__'s__ tail is long.

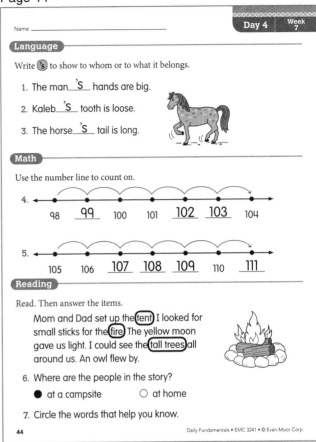

Math

Use the number line to count on.

4. 98 __99__ 100 101 __102__ __103__ 104

5. 105 106 __107__ __108__ __109__ 110 __111__

Reading

Read. Then answer the items.

Mom and Dad set up the (tent) I looked for small sticks for the (fire) The yellow moon gave us light. I could see the (tall trees) all around us. An owl flew by.

6. Where are the people in the story?
   ● at a campsite   ○ at home

7. Circle the words that help you know.

Page 45

Language

Write 's to show to whom it belongs. Then write to tell to whom it belongs.

1. This is his friend__'s__ bike.
   Whose bike is it?   __his friend's__
2. Mom has Sara__'s__ coat.
   Whose coat is it?   __Sara's__

Math

Count on to finish the chart. Write the numbers.

3.

101	102	103	104	105	106	107	108	109	110
111	112	113	114	115	116	117	118	119	120

Reading

Read. Then answer the items.

The bell rang and the (kids lined up) Mrs. Yang led us back to (class) It was time for (science) We each had one cup of water and one cup of sand.

4. Where are the people in the story?
   ＊__They are at school.__

5. Circle the words that help you know.

Page 46

Language

Write the word to take the place of the person.

1. Mom sits.
   __She__ sits.
   He   She
2. Tyler plays the piano.
   __He__ plays the piano.
   He   She

Math

Look at the problem. Use the picture to count on and add. Write the answer.

3. 6 + 4 = __10__

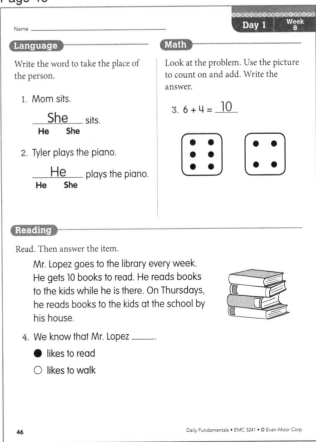

Reading

Read. Then answer the item.

Mr. Lopez goes to the library every week. He gets 10 books to read. He reads books to the kids while he is there. On Thursdays, he reads books to the kids at the school by his house.

4. We know that Mr. Lopez _____.
   ● likes to read
   ○ likes to walk

Page 47

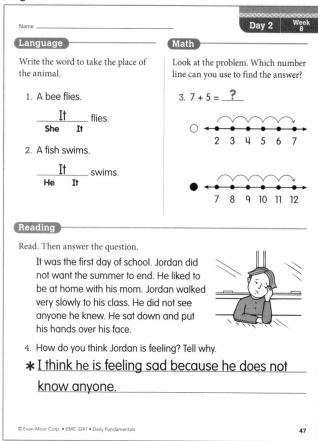

Name _____

Day 2 | Week 8

Language

Write the word to take the place of the animal.

1. A bee flies.

___It___ flies.
She   It

2. A fish swims.

___It___ swims.
He   It

Math

Look at the problem. Which number line can you use to find the answer?

3. 7 + 5 = __?__

○ (number line 2 3 4 5 6 7)

● (number line 7 8 9 10 11 12)

Reading

Read. Then answer the question.

It was the first day of school. Jordan did not want the summer to end. He liked to be at home with his mom. Jordan walked very slowly to his class. He did not see anyone he knew. He sat down and put his hands over his face.

4. How do you think Jordan is feeling? Tell why.

* I think he is feeling sad because he does not know anyone.

© Evan-Moor Corp. • EMC 3241 • Daily Fundamentals   47

Page 48

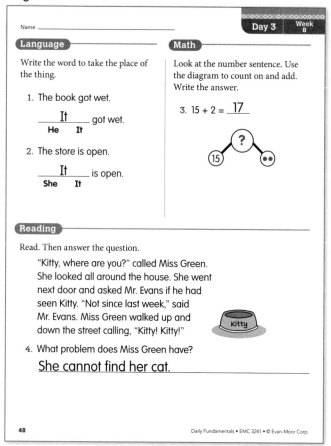

Name _____

Day 3 | Week 8

Language

Write the word to take the place of the thing.

1. The book got wet.

___It___ got wet.
He   It

2. The store is open.

___It___ is open.
She   It

Math

Look at the number sentence. Use the diagram to count on and add. Write the answer.

3. 15 + 2 = __17__

(diagram: ? with 15 and ●●)

Reading

Read. Then answer the question.

"Kitty, where are you?" called Miss Green. She looked all around the house. She went next door and asked Mr. Evans if he had seen Kitty. "Not since last week," said Mr. Evans. Miss Green walked up and down the street calling, "Kitty! Kitty!"

4. What problem does Miss Green have?

She cannot find her cat.

48   Daily Fundamentals • EMC 3241 • © Evan-Moor Corp.

Page 49

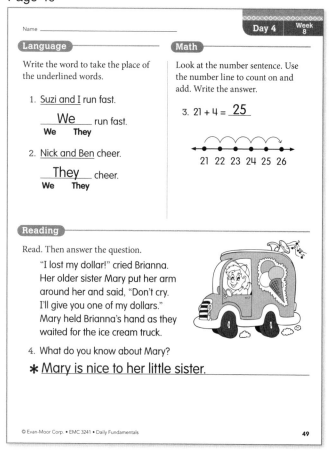

Name _____

Day 4 | Week 8

Language

Write the word to take the place of the underlined words.

1. Suzi and I run fast.

___We___ run fast.
We   They

2. Nick and Ben cheer.

___They___ cheer.
We   They

Math

Look at the number sentence. Use the number line to count on and add. Write the answer.

3. 21 + 4 = __25__

(number line 21 22 23 24 25 26)

Reading

Read. Then answer the question.

"I lost my dollar!" cried Brianna. Her older sister Mary put her arm around her and said, "Don't cry. I'll give you one of my dollars." Mary held Brianna's hand as they waited for the ice cream truck.

4. What do you know about Mary?

* Mary is nice to her little sister.

© Evan-Moor Corp. • EMC 3241 • Daily Fundamentals   49

Page 50

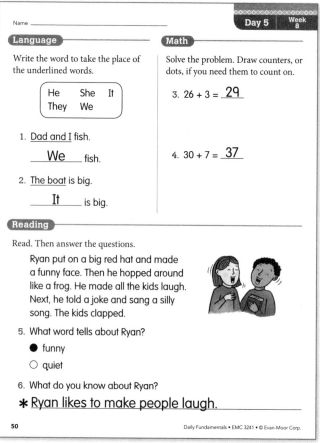

Name _____

Day 5 | Week 8

Language

Write the word to take the place of the underlined words.

| He | She | It |
| They | We | |

1. Dad and I fish.

___We___ fish.

2. The boat is big.

___It___ is big.

Math

Solve the problem. Draw counters, or dots, if you need them to count on.

3. 26 + 3 = __29__

4. 30 + 7 = __37__

Reading

Read. Then answer the questions.

Ryan put on a big red hat and made a funny face. Then he hopped around like a frog. He made all the kids laugh. Next, he told a joke and sang a silly song. The kids clapped.

5. What word tells about Ryan?

● funny
○ quiet

6. What do you know about Ryan?

* Ryan likes to make people laugh.

50   Daily Fundamentals • EMC 3241 • © Evan-Moor Corp.

Page 51

Name _____

Day 1 | Week 9

Language

Read the sentence. Is it correct? Mark **yes** or **no**.

1. The rabbit hops   ○ yes   ● no
2. The rabbits hop.   ● yes   ○ no
3. The boys read.   ● yes   ○ no
4. The boys reads.   ○ yes   ● no

Math

Count back. Write the numbers. Then pick the number that comes last.

Start here

5.

?	7	8	9	10	11	12	13	14	15

○ 16   ● 6

Reading

Read. Then answer the item.

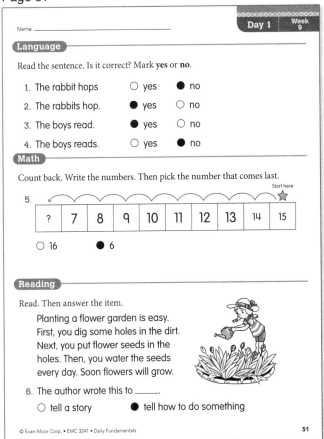

Planting a flower garden is easy. First, you dig some holes in the dirt. Next, you put flower seeds in the holes. Then, you water the seeds every day. Soon flowers will grow.

6. The author wrote this to _____.
   ○ tell a story
   ● tell how to do something

51

Page 52

Name _____

Day 2 | Week 9

Language

Read the sentence. Is it correct? Mark **yes** or **no**.

1. The boy bakes.   ● yes   ○ no
2. The boys bakes.   ○ yes   ● no
3. The girls sleeps.   ○ yes   ● no
4. The girl sleeps.   ● yes   ○ no

Math

Count back. Write the numbers.

Start here

5.

19	20	21	22	23	24	25	26	27	28

Reading

Read. Then answer the item.

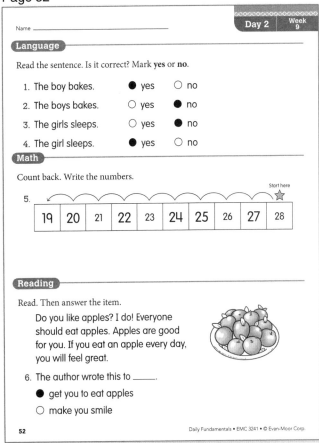

Do you like apples? I do! Everyone should eat apples. Apples are good for you. If you eat an apple every day, you will feel great.

6. The author wrote this to _____.
   ● get you to eat apples
   ○ make you smile

52

Page 53

Name _____

Day 3 | Week 9

Language

Write the correct word to finish the sentence.

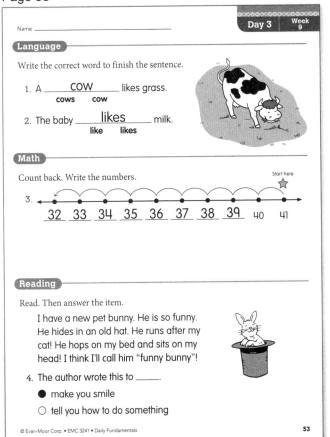

1. A ___cow___ likes grass.
   cows   cow

2. The baby ___likes___ milk.
   like   likes

Math

Count back. Write the numbers.

Start here

3.

32 33 34 35 36 37 38 39 40 41

Reading

Read. Then answer the item.

I have a new pet bunny. He is so funny. He hides in an old hat. He runs after my cat! He hops on my bed and sits on my head! I think I'll call him "funny bunny"!

4. The author wrote this to _____.
   ● make you smile
   ○ tell you how to do something

53

Page 54

Name _____

Day 4 | Week 9

Language

Write the correct word to finish the sentence.

1. Mom ___makes___ lunch.
   make   makes

2. The ___kids___ listen.
   kid   kids

Math

Count back. Write the numbers.

Start here

3.

41	42	43	44	45	46	47	48	49	50

Reading

Read. Then answer the item.

We can see the moon. It is smaller than Earth. The moon has no air. No people or plants live there.

4. The author wrote this to _____.
   ○ get you to do something
   ● tell you about something

54

Page 55

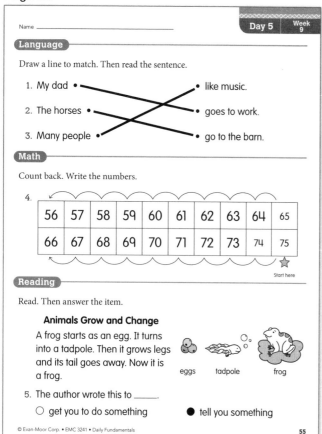

Name _____

Day 5 | Week 9

Language

Draw a line to match. Then read the sentence.

1. My dad •   • like music.
2. The horses •   • goes to work.
3. Many people •   • go to the barn.

Math

Count back. Write the numbers.

4.

56	57	58	59	60	61	62	63	64	65
66	67	68	69	70	71	72	73	74	75

Start here

Reading

Read. Then answer the item.

Animals Grow and Change

A frog starts as an egg. It turns into a tadpole. Then it grows legs and its tail goes away. Now it is a frog.

eggs   tadpole   frog

5. The author wrote this to _____.

○ get you to do something   ● tell you something

© Evan-Moor Corp. • EMC 3241 • Daily Fundamentals   55

Page 56

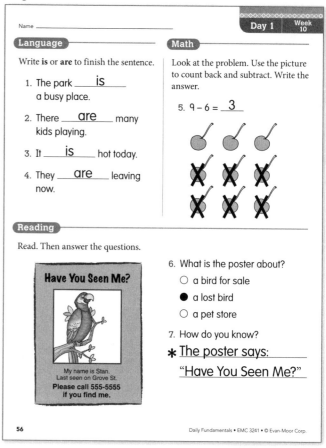

Name _____

Day 1 | Week 10

Language

Write **is** or **are** to finish the sentence.

1. The park ___is___ a busy place.

2. There ___are___ many kids playing.

3. It ___is___ hot today.

4. They ___are___ leaving now.

Math

Look at the problem. Use the picture to count back and subtract. Write the answer.

5. 9 − 6 = __3__

Reading

Read. Then answer the questions.

Have You Seen Me?

My name is Stan. Last seen on Grove St. **Please call 555-5555 if you find me.**

6. What is the poster about?

○ a bird for sale
● a lost bird
○ a pet store

7. How do you know?

✱ The poster says: "Have You Seen Me?"

56   Daily Fundamentals • EMC 3241 • © Evan-Moor Corp.

Page 57

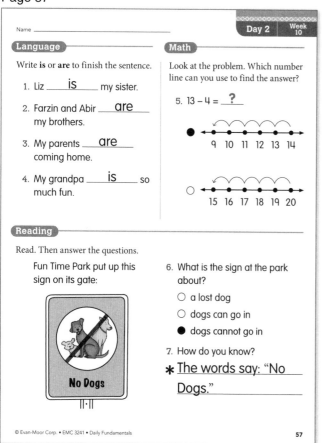

Name _____

Day 2 | Week 10

Language

Write **is** or **are** to finish the sentence.

1. Liz ___is___ my sister.

2. Farzin and Abir ___are___ my brothers.

3. My parents ___are___ coming home.

4. My grandpa ___is___ so much fun.

Math

Look at the problem. Which number line can you use to find the answer?

5. 13 − 4 = __?__

● 9 10 11 12 13 14

○ 15 16 17 18 19 20

Reading

Read. Then answer the questions.

Fun Time Park put up this sign on its gate:

No Dogs

6. What is the sign at the park about?

○ a lost dog
○ dogs can go in
● dogs cannot go in

7. How do you know?

✱ The words say: "No Dogs."

© Evan-Moor Corp. • EMC 3241 • Daily Fundamentals   57

Page 58

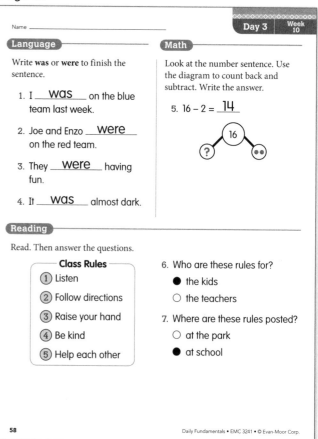

Name _____

Day 3 | Week 10

Language

Write **was** or **were** to finish the sentence.

1. I ___was___ on the blue team last week.

2. Joe and Enzo ___were___ on the red team.

3. They ___were___ having fun.

4. It ___was___ almost dark.

Math

Look at the number sentence. Use the diagram to count back and subtract. Write the answer.

5. 16 − 2 = __14__

16
? ••

Reading

Read. Then answer the questions.

Class Rules
1. Listen
2. Follow directions
3. Raise your hand
4. Be kind
5. Help each other

6. Who are these rules for?

● the kids
○ the teachers

7. Where are these rules posted?

○ at the park
● at school

58   Daily Fundamentals • EMC 3241 • © Evan-Moor Corp.

✻ These answers will vary. Examples are given.

Page 59

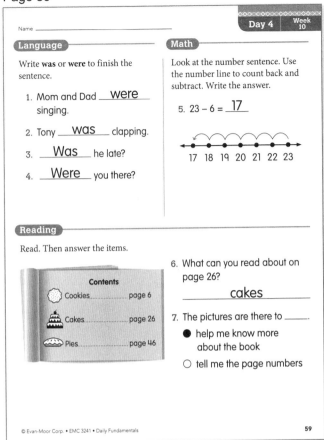

Name _____

Day 4 | Week 10

Language

Write **was** or **were** to finish the sentence.

1. Mom and Dad ___were___ singing.

2. Tony ___was___ clapping.

3. ___Was___ he late?

4. ___Were___ you there?

Math

Look at the number sentence. Use the number line to count back and subtract. Write the answer.

5. 23 − 6 = ___17___

17 18 19 20 21 22 23

Reading

Read. Then answer the items.

Contents

Cookies................page 6

Cakes...................page 26

Pies......................page 46

6. What can you read about on page 26?

___cakes___

7. The pictures are there to _____.

● help me know more about the book

○ tell me the page numbers

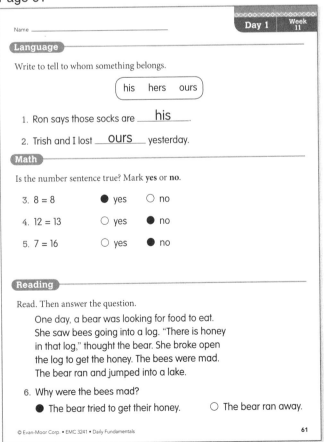

© Evan-Moor Corp. • EMC 3241 • Daily Fundamentals   59

Page 60

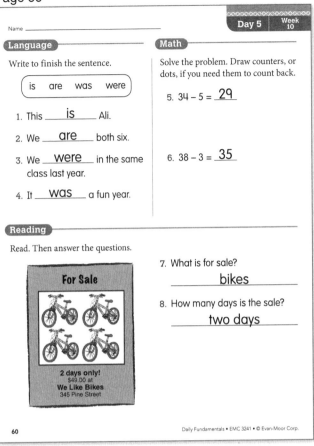

Name _____

Day 5 | Week 10

Language

Write to finish the sentence.

is   are   was   were

1. This ___is___ Ali.

2. We ___are___ both six.

3. We ___were___ in the same class last year.

4. It ___was___ a fun year.

Math

Solve the problem. Draw counters, or dots, if you need them to count back.

5. 34 − 5 = ___29___

6. 38 − 3 = ___35___

Reading

Read. Then answer the questions.

For Sale

2 days only!
$49.00 at
We Like Bikes
345 Pine Street

7. What is for sale?

___bikes___

8. How many days is the sale?

___two days___

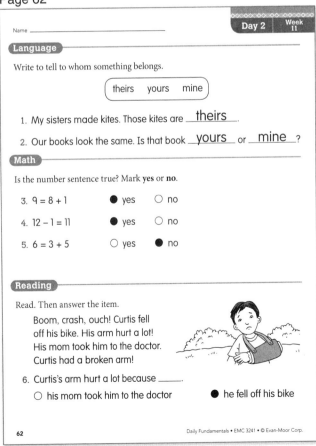

60   Daily Fundamentals • EMC 3241 • © Evan-Moor Corp.

Page 61

Name _____

Day 1 | Week 11

Language

Write to tell to whom something belongs.

his   hers   ours

1. Ron says those socks are ___his___.

2. Trish and I lost ___ours___ yesterday.

Math

Is the number sentence true? Mark **yes** or **no**.

3. 8 = 8   ● yes   ○ no

4. 12 = 13   ○ yes   ● no

5. 7 = 16   ○ yes   ● no

Reading

Read. Then answer the question.

One day, a bear was looking for food to eat. She saw bees going into a log. "There is honey in that log," thought the bear. She broke open the log to get the honey. The bees were mad. The bear ran and jumped into a lake.

6. Why were the bees mad?

● The bear tried to get their honey.   ○ The bear ran away.

© Evan-Moor Corp. • EMC 3241 • Daily Fundamentals   61

Page 62

Name _____

Day 2 | Week 11

Language

Write to tell to whom something belongs.

theirs   yours   mine

1. My sisters made kites. Those kites are ___theirs___.

2. Our books look the same. Is that book ___yours___ or ___mine___?

Math

Is the number sentence true? Mark **yes** or **no**.

3. 9 = 8 + 1   ● yes   ○ no

4. 12 − 1 = 11   ● yes   ○ no

5. 6 = 3 + 5   ○ yes   ● no

Reading

Read. Then answer the item.

Boom, crash, ouch! Curtis fell off his bike. His arm hurt a lot! His mom took him to the doctor. Curtis had a broken arm!

6. Curtis's arm hurt a lot because _____.

○ his mom took him to the doctor   ● he fell off his bike

62   Daily Fundamentals • EMC 3241 • © Evan-Moor Corp.

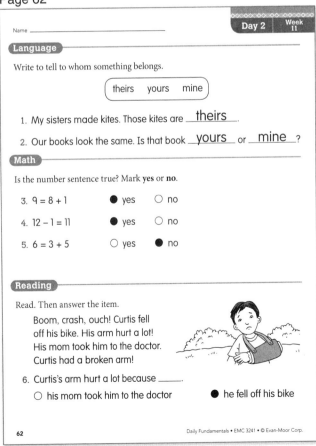

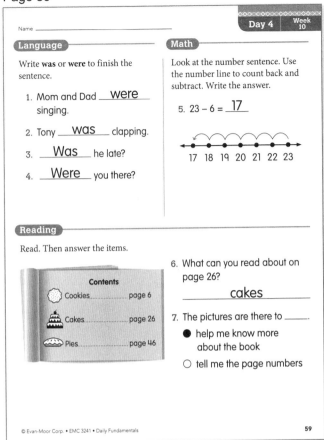

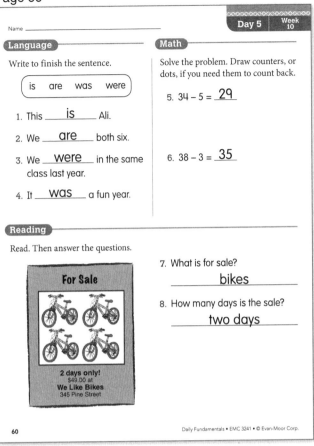

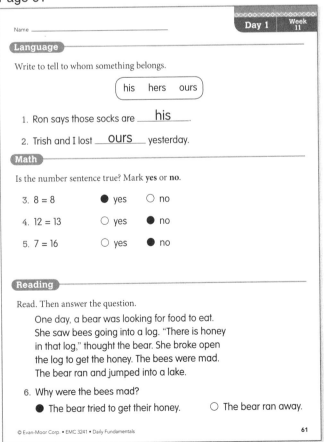

Page 63

Name _____

Day 3 | **Week 11**

Language

Write to tell to whom something belongs.

1. My mom is here. That van is ___hers___.
   theirs   hers

2. That bag belongs to me. It is ___mine___.
   mine   yours

Math

Is the number sentence true? Mark **yes** or **no**.

3. $10 - 5 = 2 + 3$ ● yes   ○ no

4. $15 - 4 = 15 - 6$ ○ yes   ● no

5. $1 + 9 = 9 + 1$ ● yes   ○ no

Reading

Read. Then answer the question.

Three little kittens lost their mittens, and they began to cry. "Oh, mother dear, we sadly fear, our mittens we have lost."

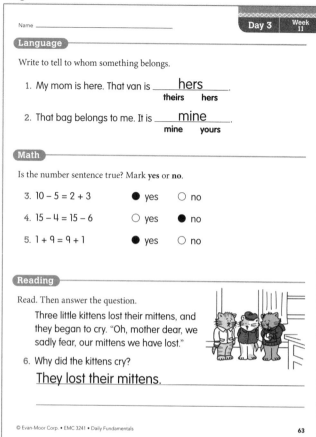

6. Why did the kittens cry?
   They lost their mittens.

© Evan-Moor Corp. • EMC 3241 • Daily Fundamentals   63

Page 64

Name _____

Day 4 | **Week 11**

Language

Write a sentence using the word (mine).

*1. Mine is the red one.

Write a sentence using the word (theirs).

*2. I like theirs better.

Math

Is the number sentence true? Mark **yes** or **no**.

3. $14 - 5 = 8 + 2$ ○ yes   ● no

4. $5 + 18 = 18 + 5$ ● yes   ○ no

5. $16 + 1 = 19 - 2$ ● yes   ○ no

Reading

Read. Then answer the question.

Water can be a solid. When water gets very cold, it freezes, and it turns into a solid. Solid water is ice.

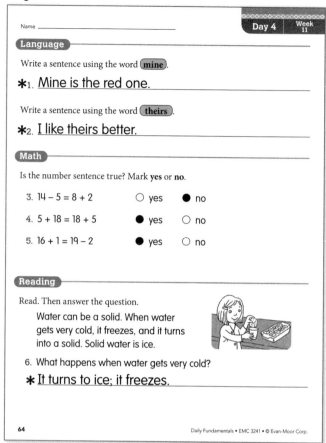

6. What happens when water gets very cold?
   * It turns to ice; it freezes.

64   Daily Fundamentals • EMC 3241 • © Evan-Moor Corp.

Page 65

Name _____

Day 5 | **Week 11**

Language

Write a sentence using the word (yours).

*1. The yellow house is yours.

Write a sentence using the word (ours).

*2. The blue house on the corner is ours.

Math

Read the word problem. Then answer the questions.

Sam ate 3 oranges, 1 apple, and 2 plums. Ben ate 3 figs, 2 pears, and 1 banana.

3. Did Sam and Ben eat the same number of fruits?   ● yes   ○ no

4. How many fruits did each of them eat?   ___6___ fruits

Reading

Read. Then answer the question.

Your body gets energy from the foods you eat. You need energy to run, to play, and to do your work. If you eat good foods, your body will have a lot of energy.

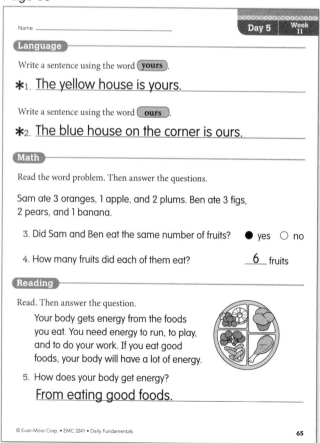

5. How does your body get energy?
   From eating good foods.

© Evan-Moor Corp. • EMC 3241 • Daily Fundamentals   65

Page 66

Name _____

Day 1 | **Week 12**

Language

Look at the picture. Circle the correct word.

1. **2**   to   (two)

2. (flower)   flour

Math

Look at the number sentence. Use the model to find the unknown number. Write the number.

3. $7 + \underline{8} = 15$

Reading

Read. Then answer the items.

Some birds fly south for the winter. They have to go where it is warm. ~~Cats like to be warm.~~ Birds find more bugs to eat in warm weather.

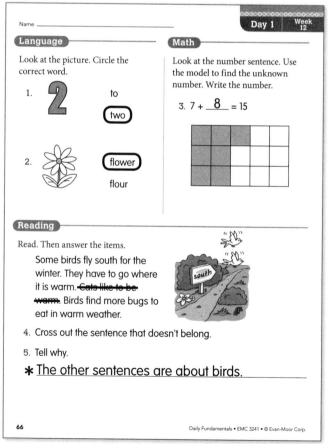

4. Cross out the sentence that doesn't belong.

5. Tell why.
   * The other sentences are about birds.

66   Daily Fundamentals • EMC 3241 • © Evan-Moor Corp.

These answers will vary. Examples are given.

Page 67

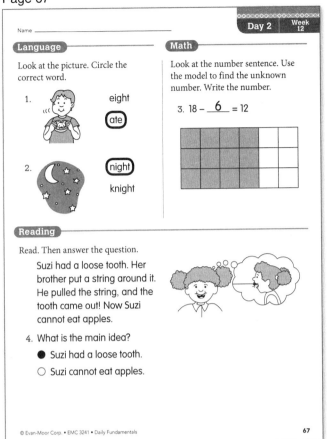

Page 68

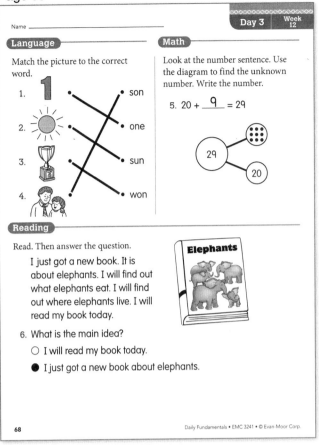

Page 69

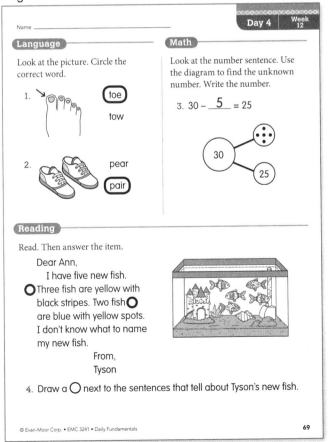

Page 70

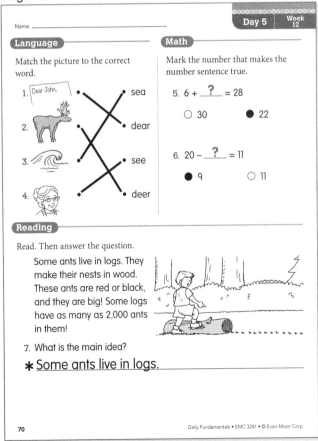

Page 71

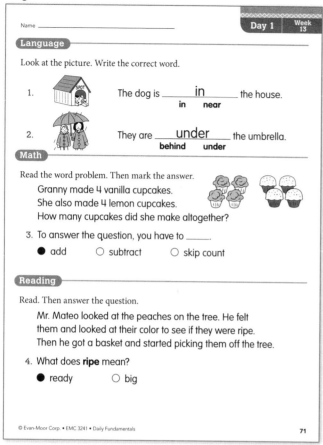

Name _____

Day 1 | Week 13

Language

Look at the picture. Write the correct word.

1. The dog is ____in____ the house.
   in   near

2. They are ____under____ the umbrella.
   behind   under

Math

Read the word problem. Then mark the answer.

Granny made 4 vanilla cupcakes.
She also made 4 lemon cupcakes.
How many cupcakes did she make altogether?

3. To answer the question, you have to _____.
   ● add   ○ subtract   ○ skip count

Reading

Read. Then answer the question.

Mr. Mateo looked at the peaches on the tree. He felt
them and looked at their color to see if they were ripe.
Then he got a basket and started picking them off the tree.

4. What does **ripe** mean?
   ● ready   ○ big

© Evan-Moor Corp. • EMC 3241 • Daily Fundamentals   71

Page 72

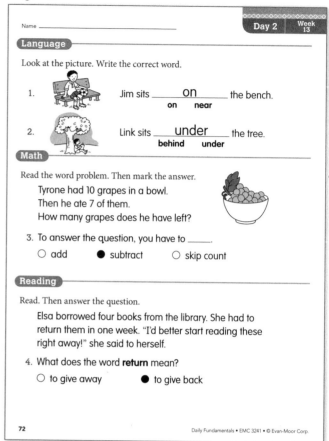

Name _____

Day 2 | Week 13

Language

Look at the picture. Write the correct word.

1. Jim sits ____on____ the bench.
   on   near

2. Link sits ____under____ the tree.
   behind   under

Math

Read the word problem. Then mark the answer.

Tyrone had 10 grapes in a bowl.
Then he ate 7 of them.
How many grapes does he have left?

3. To answer the question, you have to _____.
   ○ add   ● subtract   ○ skip count

Reading

Read. Then answer the question.

Elsa borrowed four books from the library. She had to
return them in one week. "I'd better start reading these
right away!" she said to herself.

4. What does the word **return** mean?
   ○ to give away   ● to give back

72   Daily Fundamentals • EMC 3241 • © Evan-Moor Corp.

Page 73

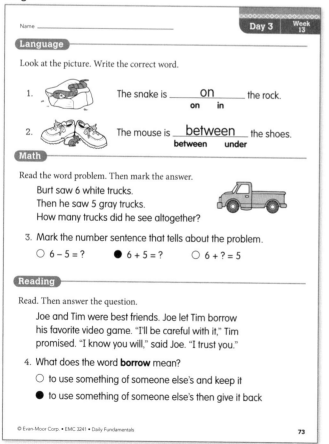

Name _____

Day 3 | Week 13

Language

Look at the picture. Write the correct word.

1. The snake is ____on____ the rock.
   on   in

2. The mouse is ____between____ the shoes.
   between   under

Math

Read the word problem. Then mark the answer.

Burt saw 6 white trucks.
Then he saw 5 gray trucks.
How many trucks did he see altogether?

3. Mark the number sentence that tells about the problem.
   ○ $6 - 5 = ?$ ● $6 + 5 = ?$ ○ $6 + ? = 5$

Reading

Read. Then answer the question.

Joe and Tim were best friends. Joe let Tim borrow
his favorite video game. "I'll be careful with it," Tim
promised. "I know you will," said Joe. "I trust you."

4. What does the word **borrow** mean?
   ○ to use something of someone else's and keep it
   ● to use something of someone else's then give it back

© Evan-Moor Corp. • EMC 3241 • Daily Fundamentals   73

Page 74

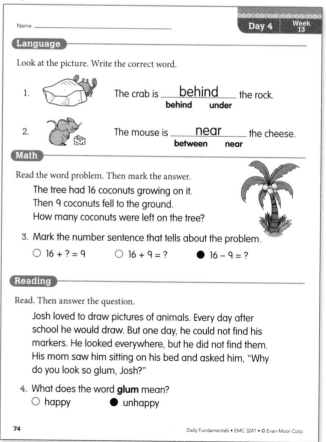

Name _____

Day 4 | Week 13

Language

Look at the picture. Write the correct word.

1. The crab is ____behind____ the rock.
   behind   under

2. The mouse is ____near____ the cheese.
   between   near

Math

Read the word problem. Then mark the answer.

The tree had 16 coconuts growing on it.
Then 9 coconuts fell to the ground.
How many coconuts were left on the tree?

3. Mark the number sentence that tells about the problem.
   ○ $16 + ? = 9$ ○ $16 + 9 = ?$ ● $16 - 9 = ?$

Reading

Read. Then answer the question.

Josh loved to draw pictures of animals. Every day after
school he would draw. But one day, he could not find his
markers. He looked everywhere, but he did not find them.
His mom saw him sitting on his bed and asked him, "Why
do you look so glum, Josh?"

4. What does the word **glum** mean?
   ○ happy   ● unhappy

74   Daily Fundamentals • EMC 3241 • © Evan-Moor Corp.

Page 75

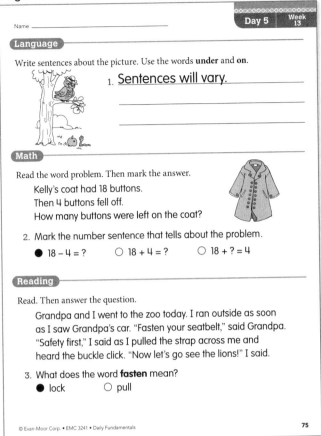

Day 5 | Week 13

Name _____

Language

Write sentences about the picture. Use the words **under** and **on**.

1. <u>Sentences will vary.</u>

Math

Read the word problem. Then mark the answer.

Kelly's coat had 18 buttons.
Then 4 buttons fell off.
How many buttons were left on the coat?

2. Mark the number sentence that tells about the problem.
   - ● 18 – 4 = ?
   - ○ 18 + 4 = ?
   - ○ 18 + ? = 4

Reading

Read. Then answer the question.

Grandpa and I went to the zoo today. I ran outside as soon as I saw Grandpa's car. "Fasten your seatbelt," said Grandpa. "Safety first," I said as I pulled the strap across me and heard the buckle click. "Now let's go see the lions!" I said.

3. What does the word **fasten** mean?
   - ● lock
   - ○ pull

© Evan-Moor Corp. • EMC 3241 • Daily Fundamentals   75

Page 76

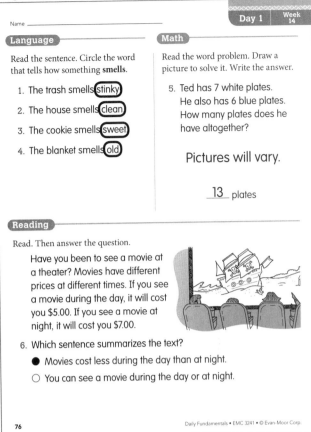

Day 1 | Week 14

Name _____

Language

Read the sentence. Circle the word that tells how something **smells**.

1. The trash smells (stinky)
2. The house smells (clean)
3. The cookie smells (sweet)
4. The blanket smells (old)

Math

Read the word problem. Draw a picture to solve it. Write the answer.

5. Ted has 7 white plates. He also has 6 blue plates. How many plates does he have altogether?

Pictures will vary.

<u>13</u> plates

Reading

Read. Then answer the question.

Have you been to see a movie at a theater? Movies have different prices at different times. If you see a movie during the day, it will cost you $5.00. If you see a movie at night, it will cost you $7.00.

6. Which sentence summarizes the text?
   - ● Movies cost less during the day than at night.
   - ○ You can see a movie during the day or at night.

76   Daily Fundamentals • EMC 3241 • © Evan-Moor Corp.

Page 77

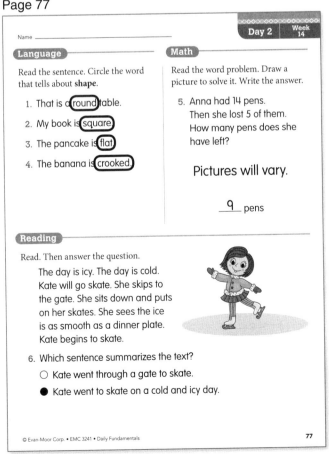

Day 2 | Week 14

Name _____

Language

Read the sentence. Circle the word that tells about **shape**.

1. That is a (round) table.
2. My book is (square)
3. The pancake is (flat)
4. The banana is (crooked)

Math

Read the word problem. Draw a picture to solve it. Write the answer.

5. Anna had 14 pens. Then she lost 5 of them. How many pens does she have left?

Pictures will vary.

<u>9</u> pens

Reading

Read. Then answer the question.

The day is icy. The day is cold. Kate will go skate. She skips to the gate. She sits down and puts on her skates. She sees the ice is as smooth as a dinner plate. Kate begins to skate.

6. Which sentence summarizes the text?
   - ○ Kate went through a gate to skate.
   - ● Kate went to skate on a cold and icy day.

© Evan-Moor Corp. • EMC 3241 • Daily Fundamentals   77

Page 78

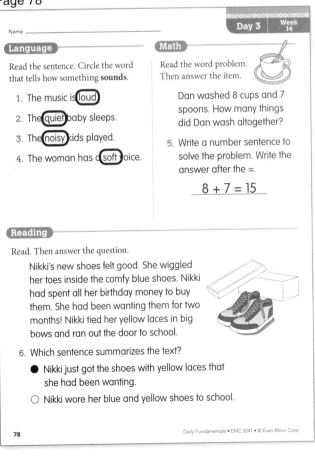

Day 3 | Week 14

Name _____

Language

Read the sentence. Circle the word that tells how something **sounds**.

1. The music is (loud)
2. The (quiet) baby sleeps.
3. The (noisy) kids played.
4. The woman has a (soft) voice.

Math

Read the word problem. Then answer the item.

Dan washed 8 cups and 7 spoons. How many things did Dan wash altogether?

5. Write a number sentence to solve the problem. Write the answer after the =.

<u>8 + 7 = 15</u>

Reading

Read. Then answer the question.

Nikki's new shoes felt good. She wiggled her toes inside the comfy blue shoes. Nikki had spent all her birthday money to buy them. She had been wanting them for two months! Nikki tied her yellow laces in big bows and ran out the door to school.

6. Which sentence summarizes the text?
   - ● Nikki just got the shoes with yellow laces that she had been wanting.
   - ○ Nikki wore her blue and yellow shoes to school.

78   Daily Fundamentals • EMC 3241 • © Evan-Moor Corp.

Page 79

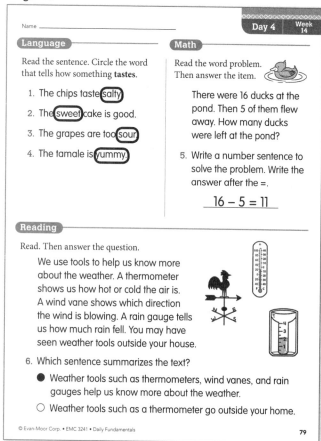

Name _____

Day 4 | Week 14

Language

Read the sentence. Circle the word that tells how something **tastes**.

1. The chips taste (salty)
2. The (sweet) cake is good.
3. The grapes are too (sour)
4. The tamale is (yummy.)

Math

Read the word problem. Then answer the item.

There were 16 ducks at the pond. Then 5 of them flew away. How many ducks were left at the pond?

5. Write a number sentence to solve the problem. Write the answer after the =.

$16 - 5 = 11$

Reading

Read. Then answer the question.

We use tools to help us know more about the weather. A thermometer shows us how hot or cold the air is. A wind vane shows which direction the wind is blowing. A rain gauge tells us how much rain fell. You may have seen weather tools outside your house.

6. Which sentence summarizes the text?

● Weather tools such as thermometers, wind vanes, and rain gauges help us know more about the weather.

○ Weather tools such as a thermometer go outside your home.

© Evan-Moor Corp. • EMC 3241 • Daily Fundamentals   79

Page 80

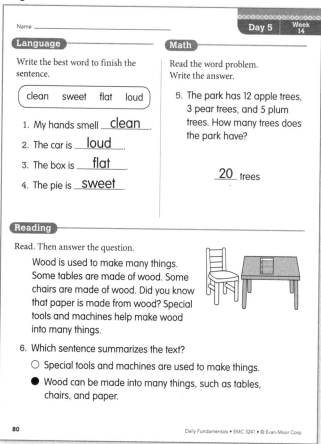

Name _____

Day 5 | Week 14

Language

Write the best word to finish the sentence.

clean   sweet   flat   loud

1. My hands smell ___clean___
2. The car is ___loud___
3. The box is ___flat___
4. The pie is ___sweet___

Math

Read the word problem. Write the answer.

5. The park has 12 apple trees, 3 pear trees, and 5 plum trees. How many trees does the park have?

___20___ trees

Reading

Read. Then answer the question.

Wood is used to make many things. Some tables are made of wood. Some chairs are made of wood. Did you know that paper is made from wood? Special tools and machines help make wood into many things.

6. Which sentence summarizes the text?

○ Special tools and machines are used to make things.

● Wood can be made into many things, such as tables, chairs, and paper.

80   Daily Fundamentals • EMC 3241 • © Evan-Moor Corp.

Page 81

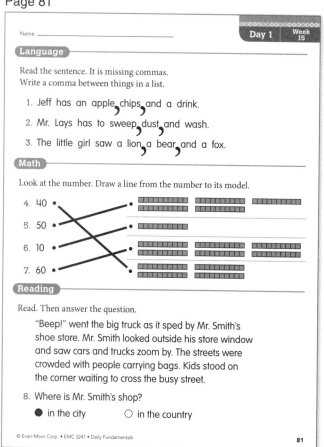

Name _____

Day 1 | Week 15

Language

Read the sentence. It is missing commas. Write a comma between things in a list.

1. Jeff has an apple, chips, and a drink.
2. Mr. Lays has to sweep, dust, and wash.
3. The little girl saw a lion, a bear, and a fox.

Math

Look at the number. Draw a line from the number to its model.

4. 40
5. 50
6. 10
7. 60

Reading

Read. Then answer the question.

"Beep!" went the big truck as it sped by Mr. Smith's shoe store. Mr. Smith looked outside his store window and saw cars and trucks zoom by. The streets were crowded with people carrying bags. Kids stood on the corner waiting to cross the busy street.

8. Where is Mr. Smith's shop?

● in the city   ○ in the country

© Evan-Moor Corp. • EMC 3241 • Daily Fundamentals   81

Page 82

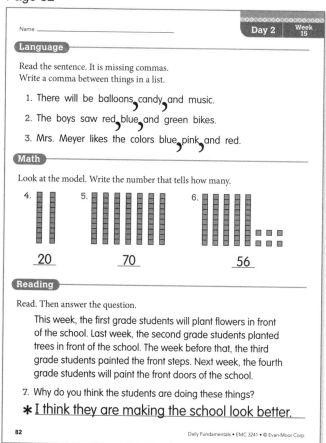

Name _____

Day 2 | Week 15

Language

Read the sentence. It is missing commas. Write a comma between things in a list.

1. There will be balloons, candy, and music.
2. The boys saw red, blue, and green bikes.
3. Mrs. Meyer likes the colors blue, pink, and red.

Math

Look at the model. Write the number that tells how many.

4. ___20___
5. ___70___
6. ___56___

Reading

Read. Then answer the question.

This week, the first grade students will plant flowers in front of the school. Last week, the second grade students planted trees in front of the school. The week before that, the third grade students painted the front steps. Next week, the fourth grade students will paint the front doors of the school.

7. Why do you think the students are doing these things?

✱ I think they are making the school look better.

82   Daily Fundamentals • EMC 3241 • © Evan-Moor Corp.

* These answers will vary. Examples are given.

Page 83

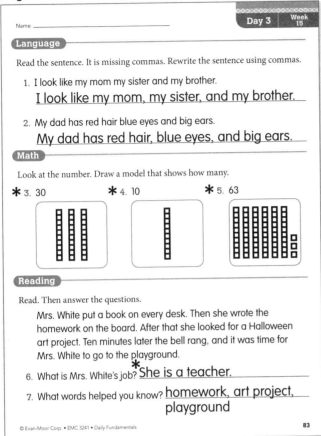

Day 3 — Week 15

Language

Read the sentence. It is missing commas. Rewrite the sentence using commas.

1. I look like my mom my sister and my brother.
   I look like my mom, my sister, and my brother.

2. My dad has red hair blue eyes and big ears.
   My dad has red hair, blue eyes, and big ears.

Math

Look at the number. Draw a model that shows how many.

*3. 30   *4. 10   *5. 63

Reading

Read. Then answer the questions.

Mrs. White put a book on every desk. Then she wrote the homework on the board. After that she looked for a Halloween art project. Ten minutes later the bell rang, and it was time for Mrs. White to go to the playground.

6. What is Mrs. White's job? *She is a teacher.

7. What words helped you know? homework, art project, playground

Page 84

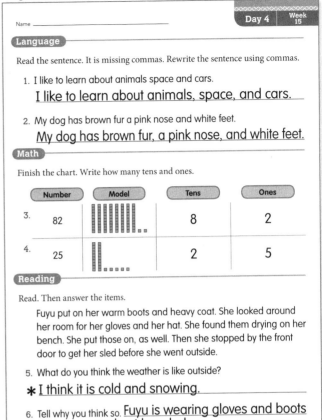

Day 4 — Week 15

Language

Read the sentence. It is missing commas. Rewrite the sentence using commas.

1. I like to learn about animals space and cars.
   I like to learn about animals, space, and cars.

2. My dog has brown fur a pink nose and white feet.
   My dog has brown fur, a pink nose, and white feet.

Math

Finish the chart. Write how many tens and ones.

Number	Model	Tens	Ones
3. 82		8	2
4. 25		2	5

Reading

Read. Then answer the items.

Fuyu put on her warm boots and heavy coat. She looked around her room for her gloves and her hat. She found them drying on her bench. She put those on, as well. Then she stopped by the front door to get her sled before she went outside.

5. What do you think the weather is like outside?
   *I think it is cold and snowing.

6. Tell why you think so. Fuyu is wearing gloves and boots and got her sled.

Page 85

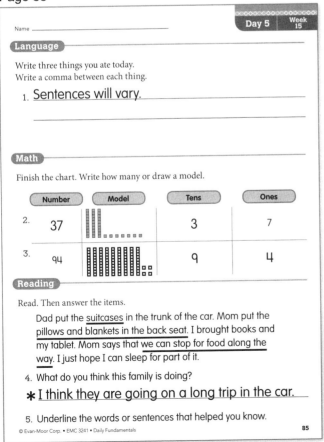

Day 5 — Week 15

Language

Write three things you ate today. Write a comma between each thing.

1. Sentences will vary.

Math

Finish the chart. Write how many or draw a model.

Number	Model	Tens	Ones
2. 37		3	7
3. 94		9	4

Reading

Read. Then answer the items.

Dad put the suitcases in the trunk of the car. Mom put the pillows and blankets in the back seat. I brought books and my tablet. Mom says that we can stop for food along the way. I just hope I can sleep for part of it.

4. What do you think this family is doing?
   *I think they are going on a long trip in the car.

5. Underline the words or sentences that helped you know.

Page 86

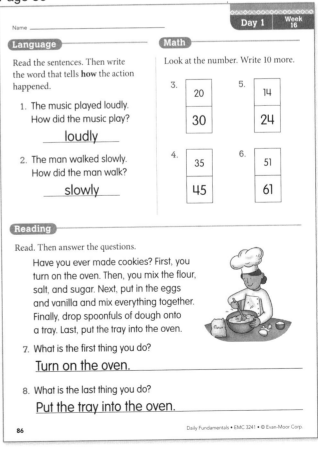

Day 1 — Week 16

Language

Read the sentences. Then write the word that tells **how** the action happened.

1. The music played loudly. How did the music play?
   loudly

2. The man walked slowly. How did the man walk?
   slowly

Math

Look at the number. Write 10 more.

3. 20 → 30   5. 14 → 24
4. 35 → 45   6. 51 → 61

Reading

Read. Then answer the questions.

Have you ever made cookies? First, you turn on the oven. Then, you mix the flour, salt, and sugar. Next, put in the eggs and vanilla and mix everything together. Finally, drop spoonfuls of dough onto a tray. Last, put the tray into the oven.

7. What is the first thing you do?
   Turn on the oven.

8. What is the last thing you do?
   Put the tray into the oven.

Page 87

Name _____

Day 2 | Week 16

Language

Read the sentences. Then write the word that tells **when** the action happened.

1. I go to school tomorrow. When do I go to school?

   tomorrow

2. Tracy should leave now. When should Tracy leave?

   now

Math

Look at the number. Write 10 less.

3. 80 / 90

5. 40 / 50

4. 29 / 39

6. 73 / 83

Reading

Read. Then answer the item.

We live in Aspen, Colorado. During the winter it snows a lot. Before Dad can take me to school, he has to shovel the snow off of the driveway. Then, he starts the car to warm it up. Next, he gets the snow off of the glass. Finally, we get in the car to go to school.

7. Write **1**, **2**, **3**, **4** to tell what happened.

   4 get in the car to go to school

   3 gets the snow off of the glass

   2 starts the car to warm it up

   1 shovel the snow off of the driveway

© Evan-Moor Corp. • EMC 3241 • Daily Fundamentals   87

Page 88

Name _____

Day 3 | Week 16

Language

Read the sentence. Circle the word that tells **where** the action happens.

1. Seals swim (nearby)

2. A crab swims (away)

3. I see fish (everywhere)

4. The turtle hides (inside)

Math

Look at the number. Write ten more and ten less.

5.

less		more
36	46	56

6.

less		more
77	87	97

Reading

Read. Then answer the items.

Can It Be Fixed?

1. Nico's dad fixed his toy.
2. Nico's toy broke.
3. Nico asked his dad to fix his toy.
4. Now Nico can play with his toy again.

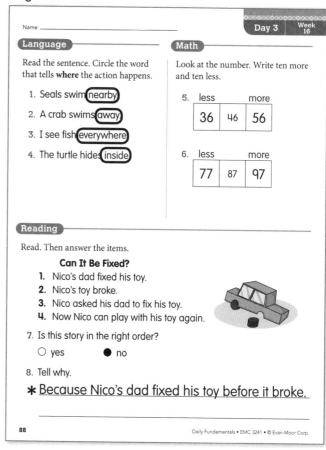

7. Is this story in the right order?

   ○ yes   ● no

8. Tell why.

   ✱ **Because Nico's dad fixed his toy before it broke.**

88   Daily Fundamentals • EMC 3241 • © Evan-Moor Corp.

Page 89

Name _____

Day 4 | Week 16

Language

Write **ly** to make the word an adverb. Then read the sentence.

1. Diana cuts careful **ly**.
2. Scott writes neat **ly**.
3. Kim walks slow **ly**.
4. Ben moves quick **ly**.

Math

Read the word problem. Write the answer.

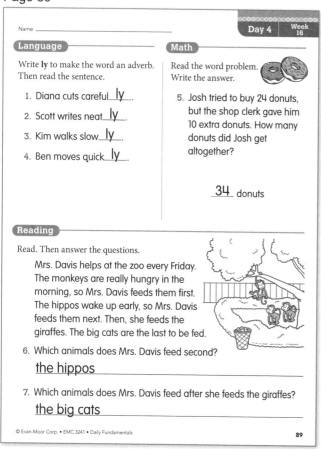

5. Josh tried to buy 24 donuts, but the shop clerk gave him 10 extra donuts. How many donuts did Josh get altogether?

   34 donuts

Reading

Read. Then answer the questions.

Mrs. Davis helps at the zoo every Friday. The monkeys are really hungry in the morning, so Mrs. Davis feeds them first. The hippos wake up early, so Mrs. Davis feeds them next. Then, she feeds the giraffes. The big cats are the last to be fed.

6. Which animals does Mrs. Davis feed second?

   the hippos

7. Which animals does Mrs. Davis feed after she feeds the giraffes?

   the big cats

© Evan-Moor Corp. • EMC 3241 • Daily Fundamentals   89

Page 90

Name _____

Day 5 | Week 16

Language

Write **ly** to make the word an adverb. Then read the sentence.

1. The men cheered loud **ly**.
2. The boy rides quick **ly**.

Write an adverb.

3. **Answers will vary.**

Math

Read the word problem. Write the answer.

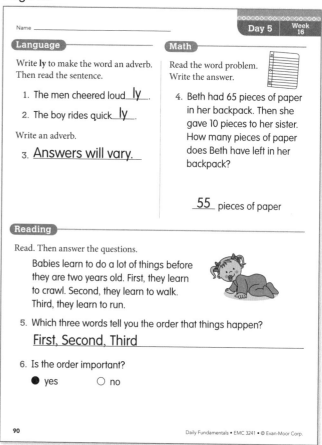

4. Beth had 65 pieces of paper in her backpack. Then she gave 10 pieces to her sister. How many pieces of paper does Beth have left in her backpack?

   55 pieces of paper

Reading

Read. Then answer the questions.

Babies learn to do a lot of things before they are two years old. First, they learn to crawl. Second, they learn to walk. Third, they learn to run.

5. Which three words tell you the order that things happen?

   First, Second, Third

6. Is the order important?

   ● yes   ○ no

90   Daily Fundamentals • EMC 3241 • © Evan-Moor Corp.

These answers will vary. Examples are given.

Page 91

Language

Circle the part of the sentence that tells **who** or **what** the sentence talks about.

1. (The class) worked at their desks.
2. (The teacher) rang the bell.
3. (The fish) swam in their bowl.

Math

Look at each number and the model below it. Then write <, =, or > in the ◯ to make a true number sentence.

4. 42 (=) 42

5. 75 (>) 67

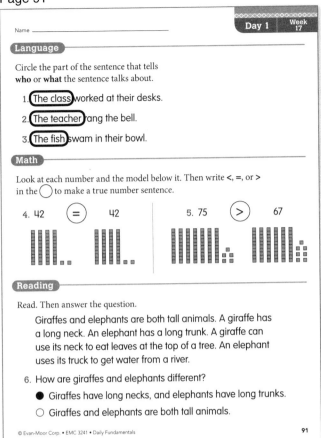

Reading

Read. Then answer the question.

Giraffes and elephants are both tall animals. A giraffe has a long neck. An elephant has a long trunk. A giraffe can use its neck to eat leaves at the top of a tree. An elephant uses its truck to get water from a river.

6. How are giraffes and elephants different?
   - ● Giraffes have long necks, and elephants have long trunks.
   - ◯ Giraffes and elephants are both tall animals.

Page 92

Language

Circle the part of the sentence that tells **who** or **what** the sentence talks about.

1. (The people) lined up for the ride.
2. (Many children) laughed and smiled.
3. (The small monkey) danced a jig.

Math

Write <, =, or > in the ◯ to make a true number sentence.

4. 17 (<) 23
6. 36 (=) 36

5. 84 (>) 48
7. 53 (<) 54

Reading

Read. Then answer the question.

Have you ever gone on a trip to a place that is far from your home? Some people ride planes or trains when they travel. Both trains and planes can fit a lot of people. Trains travel on land. Planes travel by air. Both planes and trains have wheels.

8. How are planes and trains the same?
   - ◯ They both travel by land and air.
   - ● They both have wheels, and they both can fit a lot of people.

Page 93

Language

Circle the part of the sentence that tells **what happens**.

1. My friend Will (lost his tooth)
2. The baker (made cookies)
3. The man (helped a cat)

Math

Look at the number sentence. Then mark the number that will make it true.

4. 33 = __?__   ● 33   ◯ 59
5. 12 > __?__   ● 11   ◯ 21
6. 70 < __?__   ◯ 68   ● 73

Reading

Read. Then answer the item.

Plants and animals live in oceans. Plants and animals also live in deserts. Oceans are wet. Deserts are dry. But both oceans and deserts have sand.

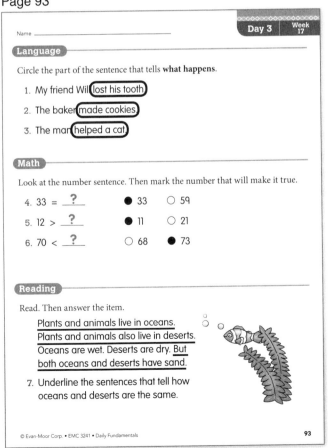

7. Underline the sentences that tell how oceans and deserts are the same.

Page 94

Language

Circle the part of the sentence that tells **what happens**.

1. Lisa always (wakes up at 7 a.m.)
2. The police officer (rides a bike)
3. Blanca (likes to color)

Math

Look at the number sentence. Write a two-digit number to complete it.

*4. 89 < 92
5. 45 = 45
*6. 13 > 10

*7. 60 > 27
*8. 52 < 61
9. 99 = 99

Reading

Read. Then answer the items.

Tran and his sister Lan do not go to bed at the same time. Tran is older than Lan. But both Tran and Lan brush their teeth and wash their face and hands before bed. Both of them also kiss their parents before bed. ◯ ◯

10. Underline the sentences that tell how Tran and Lan are different.

11. Draw a ◯ next to the sentences that tell how they are the same.

These answers will vary. Examples are given.

Page 95

Language

Write the part of the sentence that tells **what happens**.

1. Yesterday Ann _____ Answers will vary.

2. Today Tom will _____

3. Tomorrow Logan _____

Math

Read the word problem. Then answer the items.

Toya can sing 48 songs. Eddie can sing 51 songs. Who can sing more songs?

4. Who can sing more songs? _____ Eddie

5. Write a number sentence about the problem. Use <, =, or >.

$48 < 51$

Reading

Read. Then answer the items.

Tori is going to a new school this year. <u>Her old school had 300 students. Her new school only has 100 students.</u> Both schools have art classes. Both schools have a fall festival. Tori misses her old school, but she likes her new school more every day.

6. How are Tori's old school and new school the same?

* <u>They both have art classes.</u>

7. Underline the sentences that tell how the schools are different.

Page 96

Language

Write a contraction from the word box to take the place of the two words.

[didn't   I'd]

1. _____ I'd _____ be careful.
   I would

2. You _____ didn't _____ call me.
   did not

Math

Add. Look at the models.

3. 50 + 40 = 90

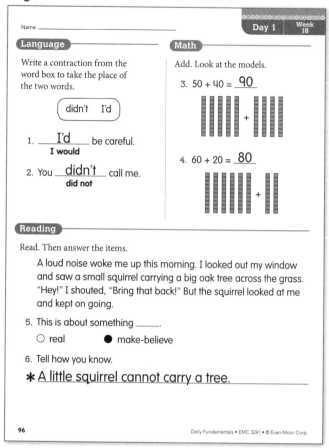

4. 60 + 20 = 80

Reading

Read. Then answer the items.

A loud noise woke me up this morning. I looked out my window and saw a small squirrel carrying a big oak tree across the grass. "Hey!" I shouted, "Bring that back!" But the squirrel looked at me and kept on going.

5. This is about something _____.
   ○ real   ● make-believe

6. Tell how you know.

* <u>A little squirrel cannot carry a tree.</u>

Page 97

Language

Write a contraction from the word box to take the place of the two words.

(can't   you'll)

1. I hope _____ you'll _____ have fun.
   you will

2. I _____ can't _____ be late.
   can not

Math

Add. Look at the models.

3. 38 + 16 = 54

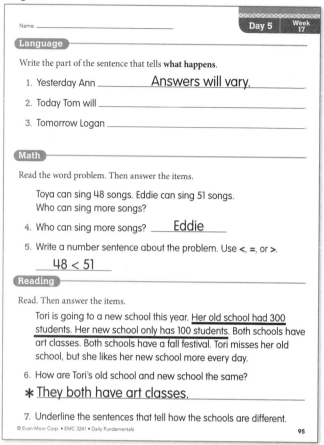

4. 64 + 25 = 89

Reading

Read. Then answer the question.

My cat Rufus always knows when I'm feeling sad. Yesterday when I got home from school, Rufus sat on my lap. When it was time for me to go to baseball practice, Rufus sat by the front window and watched me drive away.

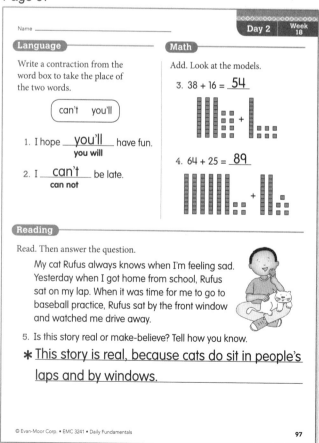

5. Is this story real or make-believe? Tell how you know.

* <u>This story is real, because cats do sit in people's laps and by windows.</u>

Page 98

Language

Write a contraction from the word box to take the place of the two words.

(aren't   shouldn't)

1. You _____ shouldn't _____ do that.
   should not

2. The kittens _____ aren't _____ sleeping.
   are not

Math

Add. Draw a model if you need it.

3. 32 + 27 = 59

Models will vary.

4. 58 + 20 = 78

Reading

Read. Then answer the question.

My soccer coach is really nice. She teaches us a lot of different ways to kick the ball. She also helps us think about the rules while we play the game. I like when she shows us how to hit the soccer ball with our heads.

5. Is this story about something real or make-believe? Tell how you know.

* <u>This is about something real, because kids have soccer coaches who teach them things.</u>

Page 99

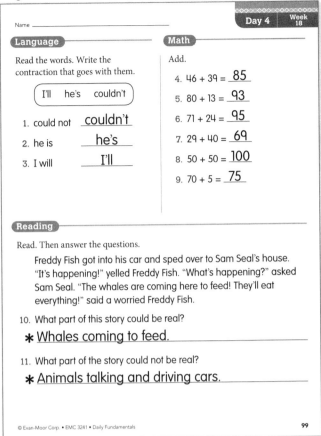

Name _____

Day 4 | **Week 18**

Language

Read the words. Write the contraction that goes with them.

| I'll he's couldn't |

1. could not ___couldn't___
2. he is ___he's___
3. I will ___I'll___

Math

Add.

4. 46 + 39 = ___85___
5. 80 + 13 = ___93___
6. 71 + 24 = ___95___
7. 29 + 40 = ___69___
8. 50 + 50 = ___100___
9. 70 + 5 = ___75___

Reading

Read. Then answer the questions.

Freddy Fish got into his car and sped over to Sam Seal's house. "It's happening!" yelled Freddy Fish. "What's happening?" asked Sam Seal. "The whales are coming here to feed! They'll eat everything!" said a worried Freddy Fish.

10. What part of this story could be real?

* ___Whales coming to feed.___

11. What part of the story could not be real?

* ___Animals talking and driving cars.___

© Evan-Moor Corp. • EMC 3241 • Daily Fundamentals   99

Page 100

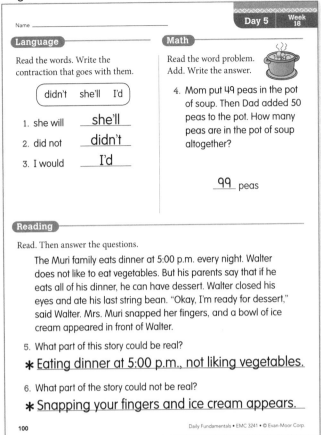

Name _____

Day 5 | **Week 18**

Language

Read the words. Write the contraction that goes with them.

| didn't she'll I'd |

1. she will ___she'll___
2. did not ___didn't___
3. I would ___I'd___

Math

Read the word problem. Add. Write the answer.

4. Mom put 49 peas in the pot of soup. Then Dad added 50 peas to the pot. How many peas are in the pot of soup altogether?

___99___ peas

Reading

Read. Then answer the questions.

The Muri family eats dinner at 5:00 p.m. every night. Walter does not like to eat vegetables. But his parents say that if he eats all of his dinner, he can have dessert. Walter closed his eyes and ate his last string bean. "Okay, I'm ready for dessert," said Walter. Mrs. Muri snapped her fingers, and a bowl of ice cream appeared in front of Walter.

5. What part of this story could be real?

* ___Eating dinner at 5:00 p.m., not liking vegetables.___

6. What part of the story could not be real?

* ___Snapping your fingers and ice cream appears.___

100   Daily Fundamentals • EMC 3241 • © Evan-Moor Corp.

Page 101

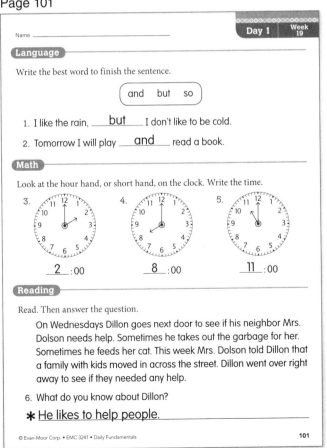

Name _____

Day 1 | **Week 19**

Language

Write the best word to finish the sentence.

| and but so |

1. I like the rain, ___but___ I don't like to be cold.
2. Tomorrow I will play ___and___ read a book.

Math

Look at the hour hand, or short hand, on the clock. Write the time.

3. ___2___ :00
4. ___8___ :00
5. ___11___ :00

Reading

Read. Then answer the question.

On Wednesdays Dillon goes next door to see if his neighbor Mrs. Dolson needs help. Sometimes he takes out the garbage for her. Sometimes he feeds her cat. This week Mrs. Dolson told Dillon that a family with kids moved in across the street. Dillon went over right away to see if they needed any help.

6. What do you know about Dillon?

* ___He likes to help people.___

© Evan-Moor Corp. • EMC 3241 • Daily Fundamentals   101

Page 102

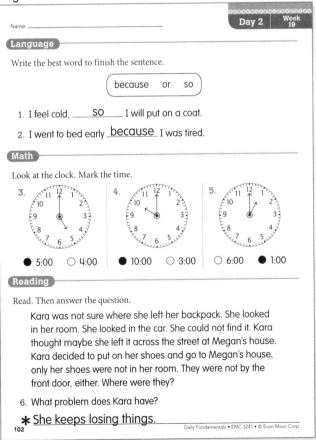

Name _____

Day 2 | **Week 19**

Language

Write the best word to finish the sentence.

| because or so |

1. I feel cold, ___so___ I will put on a coat.
2. I went to bed early ___because___ I was tired.

Math

Look at the clock. Mark the time.

3. ● 5:00 ○ 4:00
4. ● 10:00 ○ 3:00
5. ○ 6:00 ● 1:00

Reading

Read. Then answer the question.

Kara was not sure where she left her backpack. She looked in her room. She looked in the car. She could not find it. Kara thought maybe she left it across the street at Megan's house. Kara decided to put on her shoes and go to Megan's house, only her shoes were not in her room. They were not by the front door, either. Where were they?

6. What problem does Kara have?

* ___She keeps losing things.___

102   Daily Fundamentals • EMC 3241 • © Evan-Moor Corp.

Page 103

Name _____

Day 3 | Week 19

Language

Make these two sentences into one sentence.
Use the word **and** in your sentence.

1. I like grapes. I like oranges.

   I like grapes, and I like oranges.

Math

Look at the clock. Write the time.

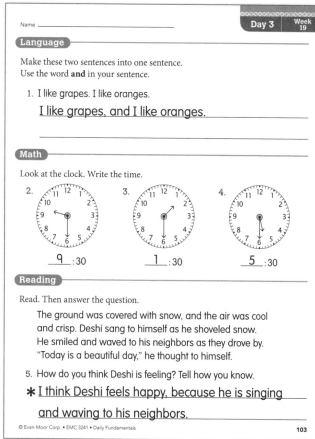

2. __9__ :30

3. __1__ :30

4. __5__ :30

Reading

Read. Then answer the question.

The ground was covered with snow, and the air was cool and crisp. Deshi sang to himself as he shoveled snow. He smiled and waved to his neighbors as they drove by. "Today is a beautiful day," he thought to himself.

5. How do you think Deshi is feeling? Tell how you know.

   * I think Deshi feels happy, because he is singing and waving to his neighbors.

Page 104

Name _____

Day 4 | Week 19

Language

Make these two sentences into one sentence.
Use the word **or** in your sentence.

1. Do you want milk? Do you want water?

   Do you want milk, or do you want water?

Math

Look at the clock. Mark the time.

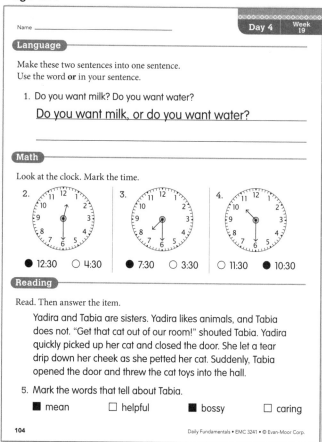

2. ● 12:30   ○ 4:30

3. ● 7:30   ○ 3:30

4. ○ 11:30   ● 10:30

Reading

Read. Then answer the item.

Yadira and Tabia are sisters. Yadira likes animals, and Tabia does not. "Get that cat out of our room!" shouted Tabia. Yadira quickly picked up her cat and closed the door. She let a tear drip down her cheek as she petted her cat. Suddenly, Tabia opened the door and threw the cat toys into the hall.

5. Mark the words that tell about Tabia.

   ■ mean   □ helpful   ■ bossy   □ caring

Page 105

Name _____

Day 5 | Week 19

Language

Make these two sentences into one sentence.
Use the word **but** in your sentence.

1. I want to buy that. I don't have any money.

   I want to buy that, but I don't have any money.

Math

Write the time. Remember to use a : in the time.

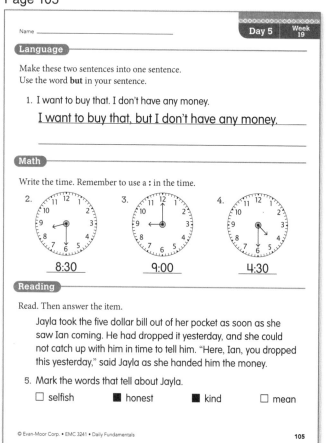

2. 8:30

3. 9:00

4. 4:30

Reading

Read. Then answer the item.

Jayla took the five dollar bill out of her pocket as soon as she saw Ian coming. He had dropped it yesterday, and she could not catch up with him in time to tell him. "Here, Ian, you dropped this yesterday," said Jayla as she handed him the money.

5. Mark the words that tell about Jayla.

   □ selfish   ■ honest   ■ kind   □ mean

Page 106

Name _____

Day 1 | Week 20

Language

Draw a line to match the words that have almost the **same** meaning.

1. big — huge
2. tiny — small
3. mad — angry
4. hop — jump

Math

Draw a line. Match the coin with its name and value.

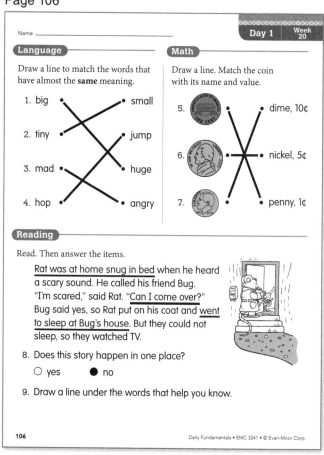

5. dime, 10¢
6. nickel, 5¢
7. penny, 1¢

Reading

Read. Then answer the items.

Rat was at home snug in bed when he heard a scary sound. He called his friend Bug. "I'm scared," said Rat. "Can I come over?" Bug said yes, so Rat put on his coat and went to sleep at Bug's house. But they could not sleep, so they watched TV.

8. Does this story happen in one place?

   ○ yes   ● no

9. Draw a line under the words that help you know.

Page 107

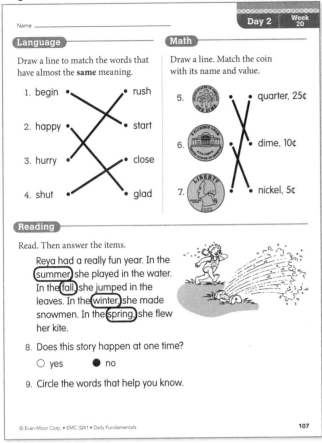

Day 2 | Week 20

Language

Draw a line to match the words that have almost the **same** meaning.

1. begin — rush
2. happy — start
3. hurry — close
4. shut — glad

Math

Draw a line. Match the coin with its name and value.

5. quarter, 25¢
6. dime, 10¢
7. nickel, 5¢

Reading

Read. Then answer the items.

Reya had a really fun year. In the (summer) she played in the water. In the (fall) she jumped in the leaves. In the (winter) she made snowmen. In the (spring,) she flew her kite.

8. Does this story happen at one time?
   ○ yes   ● no

9. Circle the words that help you know.

© Evan-Moor Corp. • EMC 3241 • Daily Fundamentals   107

Page 108

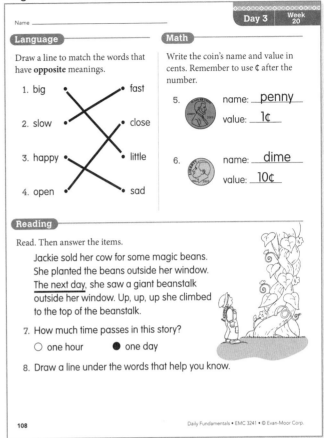

Day 3 | Week 20

Language

Draw a line to match the words that have **opposite** meanings.

1. big — fast
2. slow — close
3. happy — little
4. open — sad

Math

Write the coin's name and value in cents. Remember to use ¢ after the number.

5. name: penny   value: 1¢
6. name: dime   value: 10¢

Reading

Read. Then answer the items.

Jackie sold her cow for some magic beans. She planted the beans outside her window. The next day, she saw a giant beanstalk outside her window. Up, up, up she climbed to the top of the beanstalk.

7. How much time passes in this story?
   ○ one hour   ● one day

8. Draw a line under the words that help you know.

108   Daily Fundamentals • EMC 3241 • © Evan-Moor Corp.

Page 109

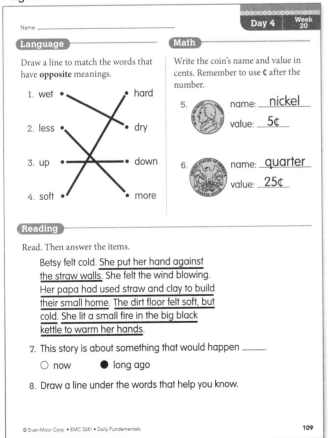

Day 4 | Week 20

Language

Draw a line to match the words that have **opposite** meanings.

1. wet — hard
2. less — dry
3. up — down
4. soft — more

Math

Write the coin's name and value in cents. Remember to use ¢ after the number.

5. name: nickel   value: 5¢
6. name: quarter   value: 25¢

Reading

Read. Then answer the items.

Betsy felt cold. She put her hand against the straw walls. She felt the wind blowing. Her papa had used straw and clay to build their small home. The dirt floor felt soft, but cold. She lit a small fire in the big black kettle to warm her hands.

7. This story is about something that would happen ____.
   ○ now   ● long ago

8. Draw a line under the words that help you know.

© Evan-Moor Corp. • EMC 3241 • Daily Fundamentals   109

Page 110

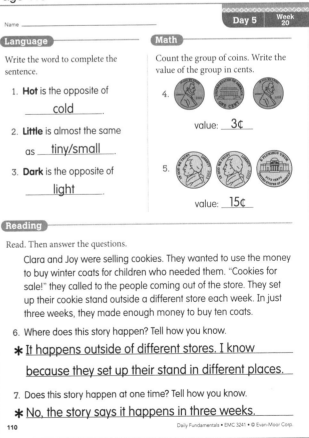

Day 5 | Week 20

Language

Write the word to complete the sentence.

1. **Hot** is the opposite of
   cold .

2. **Little** is almost the same
   as tiny/small .

3. **Dark** is the opposite of
   light .

Math

Count the group of coins. Write the value of the group in cents.

4. value: 3¢

5. value: 15¢

Reading

Read. Then answer the questions.

Clara and Joy were selling cookies. They wanted to use the money to buy winter coats for children who needed them. "Cookies for sale!" they called to the people coming out of the store. They set up their cookie stand outside a different store each week. In just three weeks, they made enough money to buy ten coats.

6. Where does this story happen? Tell how you know.
   * It happens outside of different stores. I know because they set up their stand in different places.

7. Does this story happen at one time? Tell how you know.
   * No, the story says it happens in three weeks.

110   Daily Fundamentals • EMC 3241 • © Evan-Moor Corp.

© Evan-Moor Corp. • EMC 3241 • Daily Fundamentals

185

Page 111

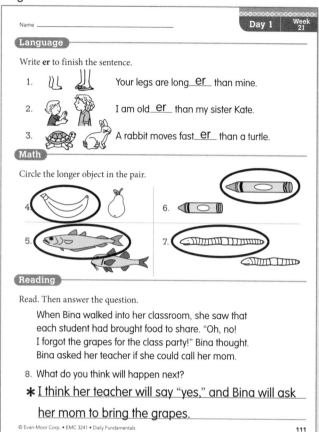

Name _____

Day 1 | Week 21

Language

Write **er** to finish the sentence.

1. Your legs are long _er_ than mine.

2. I am old _er_ than my sister Kate.

3. A rabbit moves fast _er_ than a turtle.

Math

Circle the longer object in the pair.

4. (banana) (pear)

6. (crayon)

5. (fish)

7. (worm)

Reading

Read. Then answer the question.

When Bina walked into her classroom, she saw that each student had brought food to share. "Oh, no! I forgot the grapes for the class party!" Bina thought. Bina asked her teacher if she could call her mom.

8. What do you think will happen next?

✱ I think her teacher will say "yes," and Bina will ask her mom to bring the grapes.

© Evan-Moor Corp. • EMC 3241 • Daily Fundamentals

111

Page 112

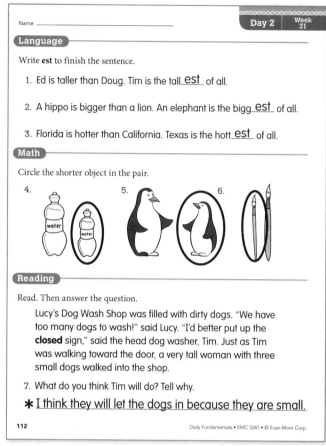

Name _____

Day 2 | Week 21

Language

Write **est** to finish the sentence.

1. Ed is taller than Doug. Tim is the tall _est_ of all.

2. A hippo is bigger than a lion. An elephant is the bigg _est_ of all.

3. Florida is hotter than California. Texas is the hott _est_ of all.

Math

Circle the shorter object in the pair.

4. (water bottles)

5. (penguins)

6. (pencil/brush)

Reading

Read. Then answer the question.

Lucy's Dog Wash Shop was filled with dirty dogs. "We have too many dogs to wash!" said Lucy. "I'd better put up the **closed** sign," said the head dog washer, Tim. Just as Tim was walking toward the door, a very tall woman with three small dogs walked into the shop.

7. What do you think Tim will do? Tell why.

✱ I think they will let the dogs in because they are small.

112

Daily Fundamentals • EMC 3241 • © Evan-Moor Corp.

Page 113

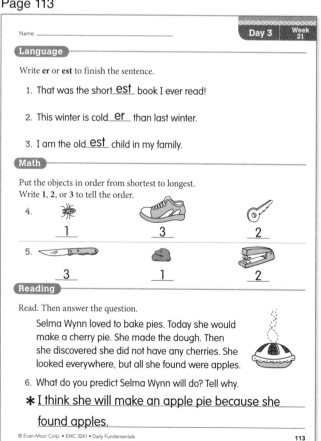

Name _____

Day 3 | Week 21

Language

Write **er** or **est** to finish the sentence.

1. That was the short _est_ book I ever read!

2. This winter is cold _er_ than last winter.

3. I am the old _est_ child in my family.

Math

Put the objects in order from shortest to longest. Write **1**, **2**, or **3** to tell the order.

4. (bug) _1_   (shoe) _3_   (key) _2_

5. (knife) _3_   (rock) _1_   (stapler) _2_

Reading

Read. Then answer the question.

Selma Wynn loved to bake pies. Today she would make a cherry pie. She made the dough. Then she discovered she did not have any cherries. She looked everywhere, but all she found were apples.

6. What do you predict Selma Wynn will do? Tell why.

✱ I think she will make an apple pie because she found apples.

© Evan-Moor Corp. • EMC 3241 • Daily Fundamentals

113

Page 114

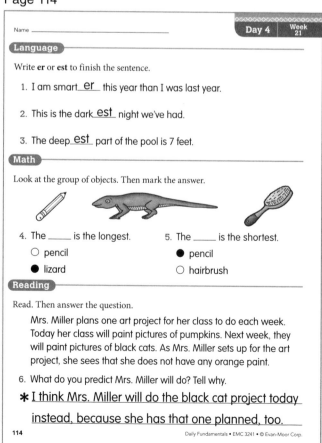

Name _____

Day 4 | Week 21

Language

Write **er** or **est** to finish the sentence.

1. I am smart _er_ this year than I was last year.

2. This is the dark _est_ night we've had.

3. The deep _est_ part of the pool is 7 feet.

Math

Look at the group of objects. Then mark the answer.

(pencil) (lizard) (hairbrush)

4. The ____ is the longest.
   ○ pencil
   ● lizard

5. The ____ is the shortest.
   ● pencil
   ○ hairbrush

Reading

Read. Then answer the question.

Mrs. Miller plans one art project for her class to do each week. Today her class will paint pictures of pumpkins. Next week, they will paint pictures of black cats. As Mrs. Miller sets up for the art project, she sees that she does not have any orange paint.

6. What do you predict Mrs. Miller will do? Tell why.

✱ I think Mrs. Miller will do the black cat project today instead, because she has that one planned, too.

114

Daily Fundamentals • EMC 3241 • © Evan-Moor Corp.

Page 115

Day 5 | **Week 21**

Name _____

Language

Write the best word to finish the sentence.

> harder   quickest   colder

1. Long words are ___harder___ to spell than short words.

2. Yesterday was cold, but today is ___colder___.

Math

Look at the group of objects. Read the sentences. Then write the answer.

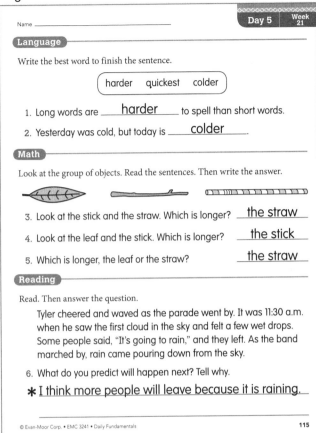

3. Look at the stick and the straw. Which is longer? ___the straw___

4. Look at the leaf and the stick. Which is longer? ___the stick___

5. Which is longer, the leaf or the straw? ___the straw___

Reading

Read. Then answer the question.

Tyler cheered and waved as the parade went by. It was 11:30 a.m. when he saw the first cloud in the sky and felt a few wet drops. Some people said, "It's going to rain," and they left. As the band marched by, rain came pouring down from the sky.

6. What do you predict will happen next? Tell why.

✱ ___I think more people will leave because it is raining.___

© Evan-Moor Corp. • EMC 3241 • Daily Fundamentals   115

Page 116

Day 1 | **Week 22**

Name _____

Language

Add . or ? to make it a sentence.

1. Where are my shoes_?_

2. Today is Friday_._

3. Have you seen Lucy_?_

4. I like ice cream_._

Math

Use the cubes to measure the object. Write the length.

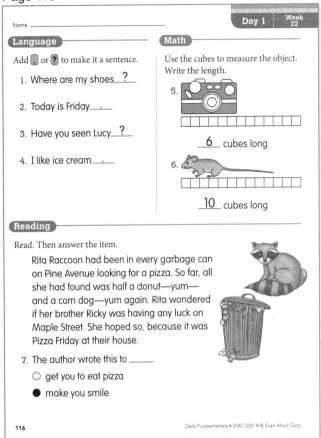

5. ___6___ cubes long

6. ___10___ cubes long

Reading

Read. Then answer the item.

Rita Raccoon had been in every garbage can on Pine Avenue looking for a pizza. So far, all she had found was half a donut—yum—and a corn dog—yum again. Rita wondered if her brother Ricky was having any luck on Maple Street. She hoped so, because it was Pizza Friday at their house.

7. The author wrote this to _____.
   ○ get you to eat pizza
   ● make you smile

116   Daily Fundamentals • EMC 3241 • © Evan-Moor Corp.

Page 117

Day 2 | **Week 22**

Name _____

Language

Add ! or ? to make it a sentence.

1. Watch out for the ball_!_

2. How are you_?_

3. That's cool_!_

4. I said stop that_!_

Math

Use the cubes to measure the object. Write the length.

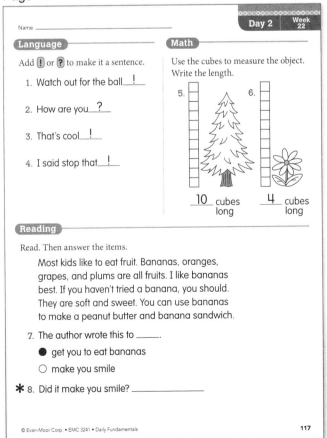

5. ___10___ cubes long

6. ___4___ cubes long

Reading

Read. Then answer the items.

Most kids like to eat fruit. Bananas, oranges, grapes, and plums are all fruits. I like bananas best. If you haven't tried a banana, you should. They are soft and sweet. You can use bananas to make a peanut butter and banana sandwich.

7. The author wrote this to _____.
   ● get you to eat bananas
   ○ make you smile

✱ 8. Did it make you smile? _____

© Evan-Moor Corp. • EMC 3241 • Daily Fundamentals   117

Page 118

Day 3 | **Week 22**

Name _____

Language

Add ! or ? to make it a sentence.

1. Hey, that's mine_!_

2. Do you know Alicia_?_

3. I'm tired now_!_

4. Are you ready to go_?_

Math

Look at the raisins to measure the object. Write the length.

5. ___5___ raisins long

6. ___4___ raisins long

Reading

Read. Then answer the question.

What's white and black and furry all over? A giant panda bear. These 300-pound bears are found in the mountains in China. A giant panda's favorite food is bamboo. In fact, most giant pandas eat bamboo 12 hours a day.

7. Why do you think the author wrote this?

✱ ___I think the author wrote this to teach people about___
  ___giant pandas.___

118   Daily Fundamentals • EMC 3241 • © Evan-Moor Corp.

Page 119

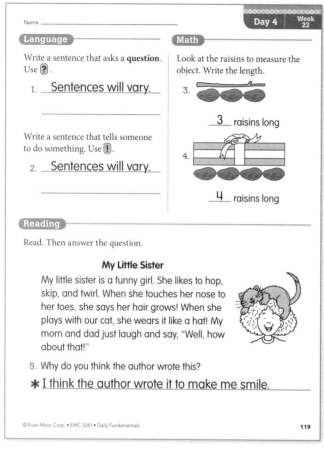

Name _____

Day 4 | **Week 22**

Language

Write a sentence that asks a **question**. Use ❓ .

1. _Sentences will vary._

_____

Write a sentence that tells someone to do something. Use ❗ .

2. _Sentences will vary._

_____

Math

Look at the raisins to measure the object. Write the length.

3. _3_ raisins long

4. _4_ raisins long

Reading

Read. Then answer the question.

My Little Sister

My little sister is a funny girl. She likes to hop, skip, and twirl. When she touches her nose to her toes, she says her hair grows! When she plays with our cat, she wears it like a hat! My mom and dad just laugh and say, "Well, how about that!"

5. Why do you think the author wrote this?

✱ _I think the author wrote it to make me smile._

© Evan-Moor Corp. • EMC 3241 • Daily Fundamentals   119

Page 120

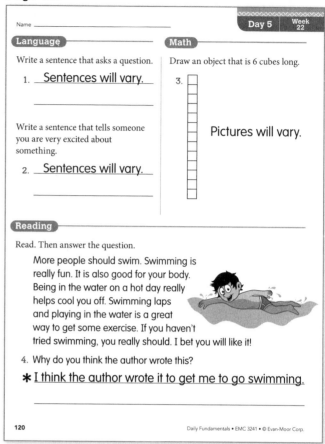

Name _____

Day 5 | **Week 22**

Language

Write a sentence that asks a question.

1. _Sentences will vary._

_____

Write a sentence that tells someone you are very excited about something.

2. _Sentences will vary._

Math

Draw an object that is 6 cubes long.

3.

Pictures will vary.

Reading

Read. Then answer the question.

More people should swim. Swimming is really fun. It is also good for your body. Being in the water on a hot day really helps cool you off. Swimming laps and playing in the water is a great way to get some exercise. If you haven't tried swimming, you really should. I bet you will like it!

4. Why do you think the author wrote this?

✱ _I think the author wrote it to get me to go swimming._

_____

120   Daily Fundamentals • EMC 3241 • © Evan-Moor Corp.

Page 121

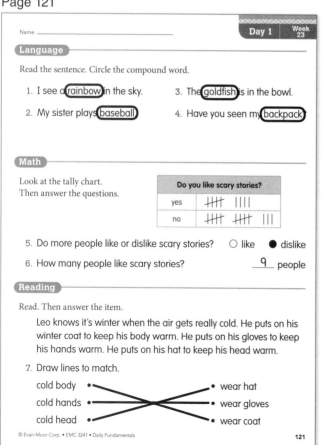

Name _____

Day 1 | **Week 23**

Language

Read the sentence. Circle the compound word.

1. I see a (rainbow) in the sky.

2. My sister plays (baseball)

3. The (goldfish) is in the bowl.

4. Have you seen my (backpack)

Math

Look at the tally chart. Then answer the questions.

Do you like scary stories?	
yes	卌 IIII
no	卌 卌 III

5. Do more people like or dislike scary stories?   ○ like   ● dislike

6. How many people like scary stories?   _9_ people

Reading

Read. Then answer the item.

Leo knows it's winter when the air gets really cold. He puts on his winter coat to keep his body warm. He puts on his gloves to keep his hands warm. He puts on his hat to keep his head warm.

7. Draw lines to match.

cold body • ———————— • wear hat
cold hands • ———————— • wear gloves
cold head • ———————— • wear coat

© Evan-Moor Corp. • EMC 3241 • Daily Fundamentals   121

Page 122

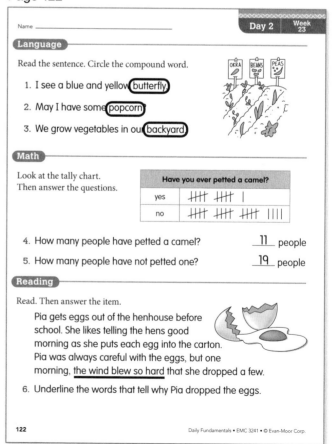

Name _____

Day 2 | **Week 23**

Language

Read the sentence. Circle the compound word.

1. I see a blue and yellow (butterfly)

2. May I have some (popcorn)

3. We grow vegetables in our (backyard)

Math

Look at the tally chart. Then answer the questions.

Have you ever petted a camel?	
yes	卌 卌 I
no	卌 卌 卌 IIII

4. How many people have petted a camel?   _11_ people

5. How many people have not petted one?   _19_ people

Reading

Read. Then answer the item.

Pia gets eggs out of the henhouse before school. She likes telling the hens good morning as she puts each egg into the carton. Pia was always careful with the eggs, but one morning, the wind blew so hard that she dropped a few.

6. Underline the words that tell why Pia dropped the eggs.

122   Daily Fundamentals • EMC 3241 • © Evan-Moor Corp.

Page 123

Name _____

Day 3 | Week 23

Language

Match the words to make a compound word.
Then write the compound word you made.

1. camp • ⟋ • fish   campfire
2. bed • ⟋ • fire   bedroom
3. jelly • ⟋ • cake   jellyfish
4. cup • • room   cupcake

Math

Look at the tally chart.
Then answer the questions.

How many did people see at the park?	
deer	＼＼＼＼ ＼＼＼＼ ＼＼＼＼ ＼＼＼＼ ＼＼＼＼ ＼
rabbits	＼＼＼＼ ＼＼＼＼ ＼

5. What animal did people see more of?   deer

6. How many more?   15 more

Reading

Read. Then answer the item.

Plants need heat and light to grow.
When spring comes, plants get
more heat and light. Some places
get a lot of rain in spring. The rain
helps plants grow, too.

7. Mark the things that help plants grow.

■ heat   ■ rain   ■ spring   ☐ places

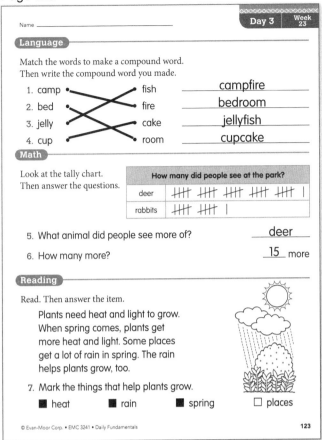

© Evan-Moor Corp. • EMC 3241 • Daily Fundamentals   123

Page 124

Name _____

Day 4 | Week 23

Language

Match the words to make a compound word.
Then write the compound word you made.

1. pan • • ball   pancake
2. rain • • bow   rainbow
3. sea • • cake   seashell
4. foot • • shell   football

Math

Look at the tally chart.
Then answer the questions.

What do you usually have for breakfast?	
eggs	＼＼＼＼ ＼＼＼＼ ＼＼＼＼
cereal	＼＼＼＼ ＼＼＼＼ ＼＼＼＼ ＼＼＼＼
toast	＼＼＼＼ ＼＼＼＼

5. How many people told what they eat for breakfast?   45 people

6. What do most people eat for breakfast?   cereal

Reading

Read. Then answer the question.

Ming reads a book before bed each night. But
sometimes she falls asleep before she finishes
reading! When this happens, she wakes up an hour early
the next morning. Then she feels tired all day at school.

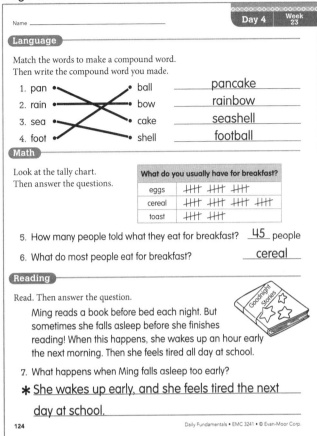

7. What happens when Ming falls asleep too early?

✱ She wakes up early, and she feels tired the next
day at school.

124   Daily Fundamentals • EMC 3241 • © Evan-Moor Corp.

Page 125

Name _____

Day 5 | Week 23

Language

Use the word box to make compound words.

tooth	bath	sun	corn
tub	brush	pop	shine

1. toothbrush   3. sunshine
2. bathtub   4. popcorn

Math

Read the word problem. Then answer the items.

In my class, 17 students have brown
hair, 14 students have black hair, and
9 students have red hair.

Students' Hair Color	
brown	＼＼＼＼ ＼＼＼＼ ＼＼＼＼ ＼＼
black	＼＼＼＼ ＼＼＼＼ ＼＼＼＼
red	＼＼＼＼ ＼＼＼＼

5. Write tally marks in the chart to tell about the problem.

6. How many students are in the class altogether?   40 students

Reading

Read. Then answer the question.

Alex did not know why he kept losing things. He put a piece
of candy in his pocket, but it was gone before he could eat it.
He had also lost his good pen. It wasn't until his mom asked
him how he got a hole in his pocket that Alex understood
why he kept losing things.

7. What caused Alex to lose things?

He had a hole in his pocket.

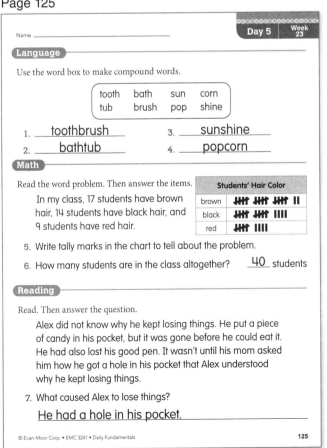

© Evan-Moor Corp. • EMC 3241 • Daily Fundamentals   125

Page 126

Name _____

Day 1 | Week 24

Language

Read the sentence. Then write **less**
or **ful** to complete the sentence.

[less   ful]

1. The care less boy
spilled milk on the floor.

2. The woman was always
care ful around fire.

Math

Look at the picture graph. Then
answer the question.

☺ or ☹ = 1 student

Do you use an eraser cap on your pencil?	
☺ ☺ ☺	☹ ☹ ☹
☺ ☺	☹ ☹
yes	no

3. Do more students use eraser
caps? Write **yes** or **no**. no

Reading

Read. Then answer the items.

Sloth

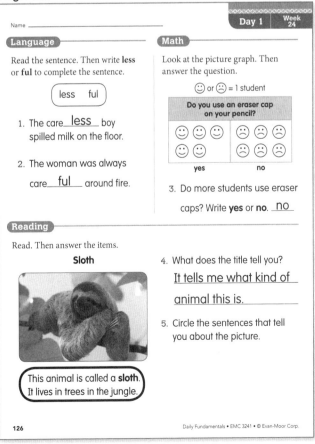

This animal is called a **sloth**.
It lives in trees in the jungle.

4. What does the title tell you?

It tells me what kind of
animal this is.

5. Circle the sentences that tell
you about the picture.

126   Daily Fundamentals • EMC 3241 • © Evan-Moor Corp.

© Evan-Moor Corp. • EMC 3241 • Daily Fundamentals   **189**

Page 127

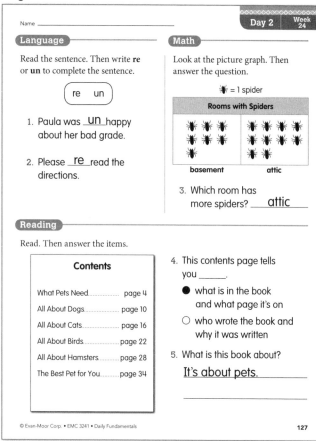

Name _____

Day 2 | Week 24

Language

Read the sentence. Then write **re** or **un** to complete the sentence.

(re   un)

1. Paula was _un_happy about her bad grade.

2. Please _re_read the directions.

Math

Look at the picture graph. Then answer the question.

🕷 = 1 spider

Rooms with Spiders	
🕷 🕷 🕷 🕷 🕷	🕷 🕷 🕷 🕷 🕷
🕷	🕷 🕷
basement	attic

3. Which room has more spiders? _attic_

Reading

Read. Then answer the items.

Contents

What Pets Need.................. page 4
All About Dogs.................... page 10
All About Cats..................... page 16
All About Birds.................... page 22
All About Hamsters............ page 28
The Best Pet for You........... page 34

4. This contents page tells you _____.
● what is in the book and what page it's on
○ who wrote the book and why it was written

5. What is this book about?
It's about pets.

© Evan-Moor Corp. • EMC 3241 • Daily Fundamentals   127

Page 128

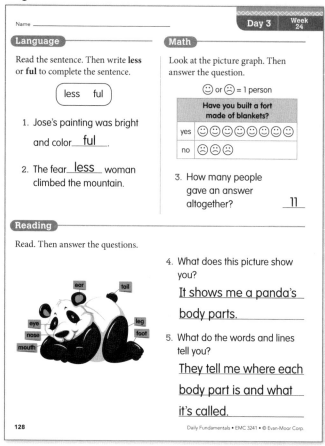

Name _____

Day 3 | Week 24

Language

Read the sentence. Then write **less** or **ful** to complete the sentence.

(less   ful)

1. Jose's painting was bright and color_ful_.

2. The fear_less_ woman climbed the mountain.

Math

Look at the picture graph. Then answer the question.

☺ or ☹ = 1 person

Have you built a fort made of blankets?	
yes	☺☺☺☺☺☺☺☺
no	☹☹☹

3. How many people gave an answer altogether? _11_

Reading

Read. Then answer the questions.

[panda diagram with labels: ear, tail, eye, nose, mouth, leg, foot]

4. What does this picture show you?
It shows me a panda's body parts.

5. What do the words and lines tell you?
They tell me where each body part is and what it's called.

128   Daily Fundamentals • EMC 3241 • © Evan-Moor Corp.

Page 129

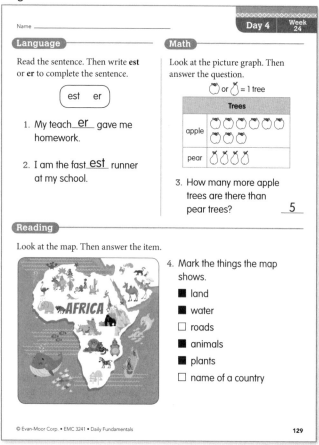

Name _____

Day 4 | Week 24

Language

Read the sentence. Then write **est** or **er** to complete the sentence.

(est   er)

1. My teach_er_ gave me homework.

2. I am the fast_est_ runner at my school.

Math

Look at the picture graph. Then answer the question.

🍎 or 🍐 = 1 tree

Trees	
apple	🍎🍎🍎🍎 🍎🍎🍎
pear	🍐🍐🍐

3. How many more apple trees are there than pear trees? _5_

Reading

Look at the map. Then answer the item.

[map of AFRICA]

4. Mark the things the map shows.
■ land
■ water
☐ roads
■ animals
■ plants
☐ name of a country

© Evan-Moor Corp. • EMC 3241 • Daily Fundamentals   129

Page 130

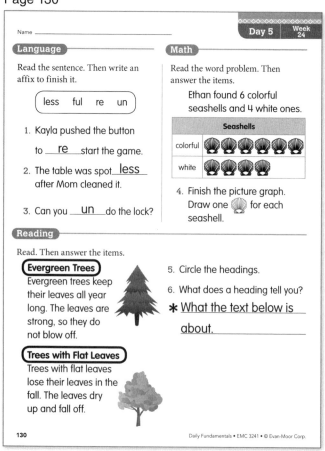

Name _____

Day 5 | Week 24

Language

Read the sentence. Then write an affix to finish it.

(less   ful   re   un)

1. Kayla pushed the button to _re_start the game.

2. The table was spot_less_ after Mom cleaned it.

3. Can you _un_do the lock?

Math

Read the word problem. Then answer the items.

Ethan found 6 colorful seashells and 4 white ones.

Seashells	
colorful	🐚🐚🐚🐚🐚🐚
white	🐚🐚🐚🐚

4. Finish the picture graph. Draw one 🐚 for each seashell.

Reading

Read. Then answer the items.

Evergreen Trees
Evergreen trees keep their leaves all year long. The leaves are strong, so they do not blow off.

Trees with Flat Leaves
Trees with flat leaves lose their leaves in the fall. The leaves dry up and fall off.

5. Circle the headings.

6. What does a heading tell you?
✳ What the text below is about.

130   Daily Fundamentals • EMC 3241 • © Evan-Moor Corp.

These answers will vary. Examples are given.

Page 131

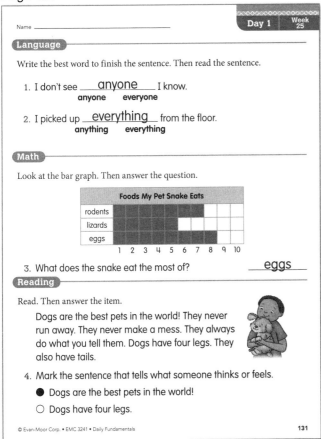

Name _____

Day 1 | Week 25

Language

Write the best word to finish the sentence. Then read the sentence.

1. I don't see ___anyone___ I know.
   anyone   everyone

2. I picked up ___everything___ from the floor.
   anything   everything

Math

Look at the bar graph. Then answer the question.

Foods My Pet Snake Eats

rodents									
lizards									
eggs									

1 2 3 4 5 6 7 8 9 10

3. What does the snake eat the most of? ___eggs___

Reading

Read. Then answer the item.

Dogs are the best pets in the world! They never run away. They never make a mess. They always do what you tell them. Dogs have four legs. They also have tails.

4. Mark the sentence that tells what someone thinks or feels.
   ● Dogs are the best pets in the world!
   ○ Dogs have four legs.

© Evan-Moor Corp. • EMC 3241 • Daily Fundamentals 131

Page 132

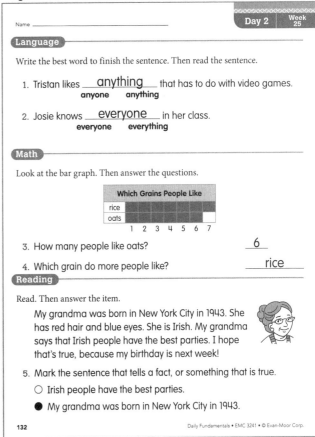

Name _____

Day 2 | Week 25

Language

Write the best word to finish the sentence. Then read the sentence.

1. Tristan likes ___anything___ that has to do with video games.
   anyone   anything

2. Josie knows ___everyone___ in her class.
   everyone   everything

Math

Look at the bar graph. Then answer the questions.

Which Grains People Like

rice							
oats							

1 2 3 4 5 6 7

3. How many people like oats? ___6___

4. Which grain do more people like? ___rice___

Reading

Read. Then answer the item.

My grandma was born in New York City in 1943. She has red hair and blue eyes. She is Irish. My grandma says that Irish people have the best parties. I hope that's true, because my birthday is next week!

5. Mark the sentence that tells a fact, or something that is true.
   ○ Irish people have the best parties.
   ● My grandma was born in New York City in 1943.

132 Daily Fundamentals • EMC 3241 • © Evan-Moor Corp.

Page 133

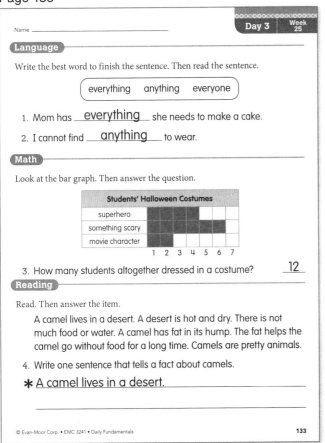

Name _____

Day 3 | Week 25

Language

Write the best word to finish the sentence. Then read the sentence.

everything   anything   everyone

1. Mom has ___everything___ she needs to make a cake.

2. I cannot find ___anything___ to wear.

Math

Look at the bar graph. Then answer the question.

Students' Halloween Costumes

superhero						
something scary						
movie character						

1 2 3 4 5 6 7

3. How many students altogether dressed in a costume? ___12___

Reading

Read. Then answer the item.

A camel lives in a desert. A desert is hot and dry. There is not much food or water. A camel has fat in its hump. The fat helps the camel go without food for a long time. Camels are pretty animals.

4. Write one sentence that tells a fact about camels.

✱ _A camel lives in a desert._

_____

© Evan-Moor Corp. • EMC 3241 • Daily Fundamentals 133

Page 134

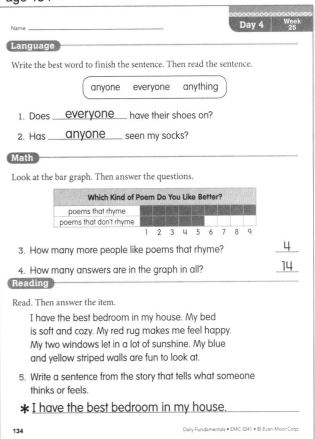

Name _____

Day 4 | Week 25

Language

Write the best word to finish the sentence. Then read the sentence.

anyone   everyone   anything

1. Does ___everyone___ have their shoes on?

2. Has ___anyone___ seen my socks?

Math

Look at the bar graph. Then answer the questions.

Which Kind of Poem Do You Like Better?

poems that rhyme								
poems that don't rhyme								

1 2 3 4 5 6 7 8 9

3. How many more people like poems that rhyme? ___4___

4. How many answers are in the graph in all? ___14___

Reading

Read. Then answer the item.

I have the best bedroom in my house. My bed is soft and cozy. My red rug makes me feel happy. My two windows let in a lot of sunshine. My blue and yellow striped walls are fun to look at.

5. Write a sentence from the story that tells what someone thinks or feels.

✱ _I have the best bedroom in my house._

134 Daily Fundamentals • EMC 3241 • © Evan-Moor Corp.

Page 135

Name _____
Day 5 | Week 25

Language

Write the best word to finish the sentence. Then read the sentence.

anyone   everyone   anything   everything

1. __Everyone__ in my family has black hair.

2. I don't think there is __anything__ left.

Math

Read the word problem. Then shade the graph to tell about the problem.

3. The bus stops at 4 schools, 7 gyms, and 9 parks.

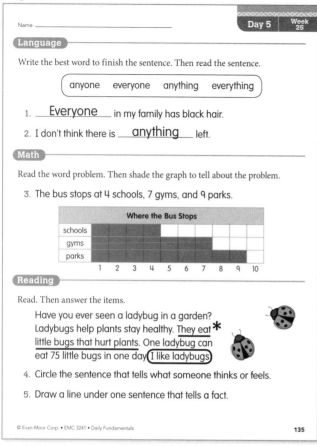

Where the Bus Stops										
schools										
gyms										
parks										
	1	2	3	4	5	6	7	8	9	10

Reading

Read. Then answer the items.

Have you ever seen a ladybug in a garden? Ladybugs help plants stay healthy. They eat ✳ little bugs that hurt plants. One ladybug can eat 75 little bugs in one day. I like ladybugs

4. Circle the sentence that tells what someone thinks or feels.

5. Draw a line under one sentence that tells a fact.

© Evan-Moor Corp. • EMC 3241 • Daily Fundamentals   135

Page 136

Name _____
Day 1 | Week 26

Language

Write the verb to tell what has **already happened**. Then read the sentence.

1. Sanji __helped__ me.
   help

2. Mr. Yin __cooked__ dinner.
   cook

3. Don __talked__ loudly.
   talk

Math

Write **2-D** or **3-D** to tell about the shape.

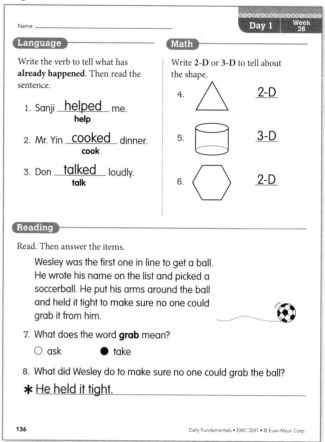

4. __2-D__

5. __3-D__

6. __2-D__

Reading

Read. Then answer the items.

Wesley was the first one in line to get a ball. He wrote his name on the list and picked a soccerball. He put his arms around the ball and held it tight to make sure no one could grab it from him.

7. What does the word **grab** mean?
   ○ ask   ● take

8. What did Wesley do to make sure no one could grab the ball?

✳ __He held it tight.__

136   Daily Fundamentals • EMC 3241 • © Evan-Moor Corp.

Page 137

Name _____
Day 2 | Week 26

Language

Write the verb to tell what has **already happened**. Then read the sentence.

1. Sally __washed__ her foot.
   wash

2. Mary __brushed__ her teeth.
   brush

3. Mike __learned__ Spanish.
   learn

Math

Draw a line. Match the object to the shape it looks like.

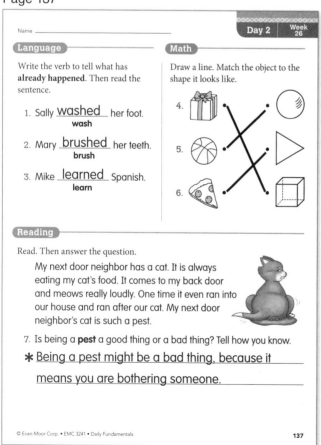

Reading

Read. Then answer the question.

My next door neighbor has a cat. It is always eating my cat's food. It comes to my back door and meows really loudly. One time it even ran into our house and ran after our cat. My next door neighbor's cat is such a pest.

7. Is being a **pest** a good thing or a bad thing? Tell how you know.

✳ __Being a pest might be a bad thing, because it__
__means you are bothering someone.__

© Evan-Moor Corp. • EMC 3241 • Daily Fundamentals   137

Page 138

Name _____
Day 3 | Week 26

Language

Write the verb to tell what **will happen**. Then read the sentence.

1. Ken __will make__ his bed.
   make

2. Izzy __will pack__ the bag.
   pack

3. Nell __will write__ a letter.
   write

Math

Draw a line. Match the object to the shape it looks like.

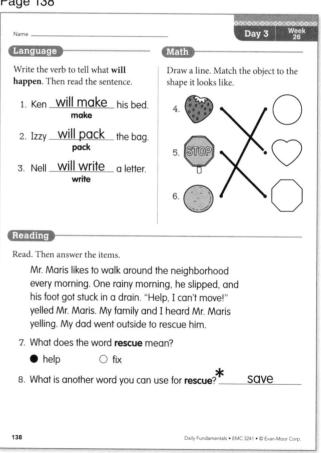

Reading

Read. Then answer the items.

Mr. Maris likes to walk around the neighborhood every morning. One rainy morning, he slipped, and his foot got stuck in a drain. "Help, I can't move!" yelled Mr. Maris. My family and I heard Mr. Maris yelling. My dad went outside to rescue him.

7. What does the word **rescue** mean?
   ● help   ○ fix

8. What is another word you can use for **rescue**? ✳ __save__

138   Daily Fundamentals • EMC 3241 • © Evan-Moor Corp.

These answers will vary. Examples are given.

Page 139

Language

Write the verb to tell what **will happen**. Then read the sentence.

1. Grandpa __will start__ the car.
   start

2. Mrs. Fields __will call__ the doctor.
   call

3. Ishmael __will fix__ the sink.
   fix

Math

Mark the name of the shape.

4. ○ triangle
   ● rectangle

5. ● circle
   ○ square

6. ● cone
   ○ cube

Reading

Read. Then answer the items.

We have a lot of pets at my house. My mom and dad both love animals. My dad finds animals that need a home. The last time my dad brought home an animal, my mom had a big grin on her face. "Perfect!" she said. "I've always wanted a pet pig!"

7. Is a person with a **grin** happy or sad?
   ● happy   ○ sad

8. What is another word you can use for **grin**? * __smile__

Page 140

Language

Read the sentence. Mark the circle that tells about it.

1. My brother will turn six this year.
   ○ already happened
   ● will happen in the future

2. I looked for my hat everywhere.
   ● already happened
   ○ will happen in the future

Math

Make a list. Write all the shapes you see in the snowman picture.

3.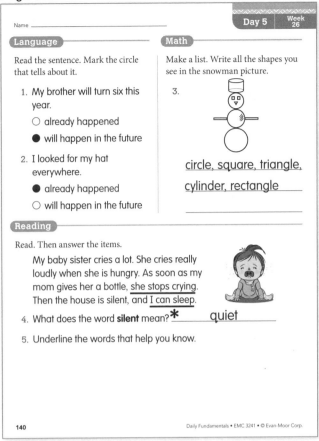

__circle, square, triangle, cylinder, rectangle__

Reading

Read. Then answer the items.

My baby sister cries a lot. She cries really loudly when she is hungry. As soon as my mom gives her a bottle, she stops crying. Then the house is silent, and I can sleep.

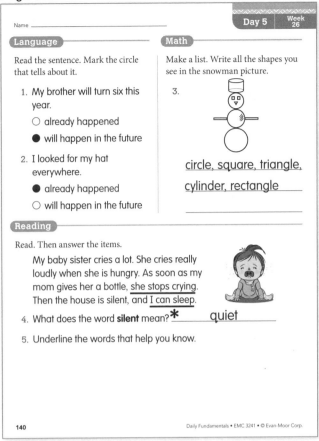

4. What does the word **silent** mean? * __quiet__

5. Underline the words that help you know.

Page 141

Language

Write the best adjective to finish the sentence.

[good   better   best]

1. Those carrots taste __good__.

2. The broccoli tastes __better__ than the carrots.

3. The string beans taste the __best__ of all.

Math

Look at the shape. Mark the answer to finish the sentence.

4.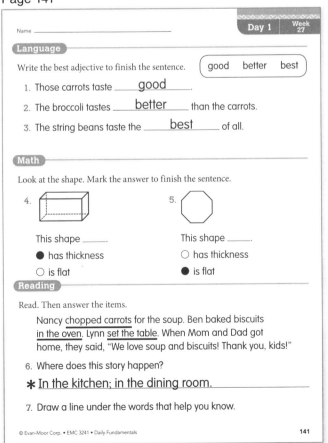
   This shape ___.
   ● has thickness
   ○ is flat

5.
   This shape ___.
   ○ has thickness
   ● is flat

Reading

Read. Then answer the items.

Nancy chopped carrots for the soup. Ben baked biscuits in the oven. Lynn set the table. When Mom and Dad got home, they said, "We love soup and biscuits! Thank you, kids!"

6. Where does this story happen?

* __In the kitchen; in the dining room.__

7. Draw a line under the words that help you know.

Page 142

Language

Write the best adjective to finish the sentence.

[bad   worse   worst]

1. Lana's cold was __bad__ today.

2. It may get __worse__ tomorrow.

3. Thursday may be the __worst__ day of all.

Math

Look at the shape. Mark the answer to finish the sentence.

4.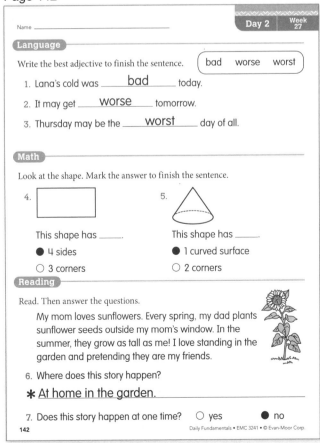
   This shape has ___.
   ● 4 sides
   ○ 3 corners

5.
   This shape has ___.
   ● 1 curved surface
   ○ 2 corners

Reading

Read. Then answer the questions.

My mom loves sunflowers. Every spring, my dad plants sunflower seeds outside my mom's window. In the summer, they grow as tall as me! I love standing in the garden and pretending they are my friends.

6. Where does this story happen?

* __At home in the garden.__

7. Does this story happen at one time?   ○ yes   ● no

⁎ These answers will vary. Examples are given.

Page 143

Name _____

Day 3 | Week 27

Language

Write the best adjective to finish the sentence.

1. There was a ___bad___ storm last night.
   bad   worst

2. All the rain will be ___good___ for the plants.
   better   good

Math

Look at the shape. Write the number of sides and corners.

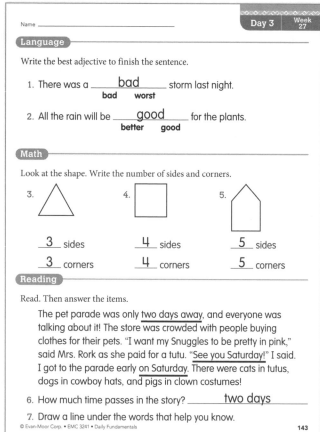

3. __3__ sides
   __3__ corners

4. __4__ sides
   __4__ corners

5. __5__ sides
   __5__ corners

Reading

Read. Then answer the items.

The pet parade was only <u>two days away</u>, and everyone was talking about it! The store was crowded with people buying clothes for their pets. "I want my Snuggles to be pretty in pink," said Mrs. Rork as she paid for a tutu. "<u>See you Saturday!</u>" I said. I got to the parade early <u>on Saturday</u>. There were cats in tutus, dogs in cowboy hats, and pigs in clown costumes!

6. How much time passes in the story? ___two days___

7. Draw a line under the words that help you know.

© Evan-Moor Corp. • EMC 3241 • Daily Fundamentals   143

Page 144

Name _____

Day 4 | Week 27

Language

Write the best adjective to finish the sentence.

1. This was the ___best___ birthday I ever had!
   best   better

2. Was it ___better___ than last year?
   best   better

Math

Look at the shape. Write the number of surfaces and corners.

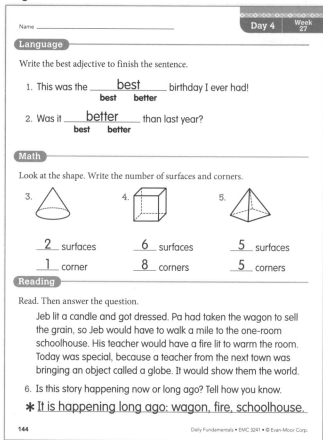

3. __2__ surfaces
   __1__ corner

4. __6__ surfaces
   __8__ corners

5. __5__ surfaces
   __5__ corners

Reading

Read. Then answer the question.

Jeb lit a candle and got dressed. Pa had taken the wagon to sell the grain, so Jeb would have to walk a mile to the one-room schoolhouse. His teacher would have a fire lit to warm the room. Today was special, because a teacher from the next town was bringing an object called a globe. It would show them the world.

6. Is this story happening now or long ago? Tell how you know.

⁎ <u>It is happening long ago: wagon, fire, schoolhouse.</u>

144   Daily Fundamentals • EMC 3241 • © Evan-Moor Corp.

Page 145

Name _____

Day 5 | Week 27

Language

| good | better | best |
| bad | worse | worst |

Write the best adjective to finish the sentence.

1. Jason is ___good/bad___ at sports.

2. Nate is the ___best/worst___ singer in our family.

3. Tasha has gotten ___better/worse___ at cleaning up.

Math

Look at the shapes. Circle shapes that have curved surfaces. Draw a box around shapes that have flat surfaces. HINT: Some shapes have both.

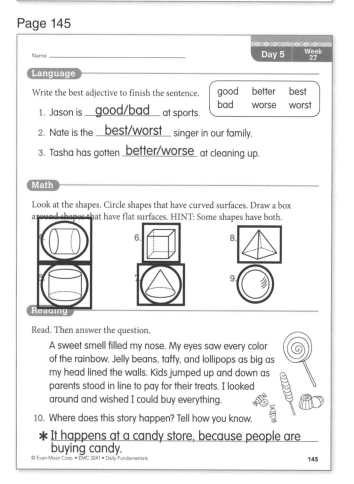

Reading

Read. Then answer the question.

A sweet smell filled my nose. My eyes saw every color of the rainbow. Jelly beans, taffy, and lollipops as big as my head lined the walls. Kids jumped up and down as parents stood in line to pay for their treats. I looked around and wished I could buy everything.

10. Where does this story happen? Tell how you know.

⁎ <u>It happens at a candy store, because people are</u> <u>buying candy.</u>

© Evan-Moor Corp. • EMC 3241 • Daily Fundamentals   145

Page 146

Name _____

Day 1 | Week 28

Language

Read the sentence. Write the correct word to finish the sentence.

1. May I have ___two___ chips?
   to   two

2. Raj went ___to___ school.
   to   two

3. My brother is ___two___ years old.
   to   two

Math

Circle the two shapes that can be used to make the bigger shape.

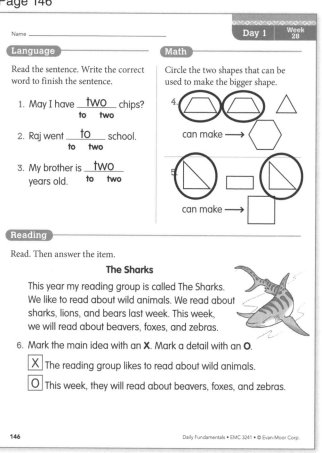

4. can make ⟶

5. can make ⟶

Reading

Read. Then answer the item.

The Sharks

This year my reading group is called The Sharks. We like to read about wild animals. We read about sharks, lions, and bears last week. This week, we will read about beavers, foxes, and zebras.

6. Mark the main idea with an **X**. Mark a detail with an **O**.

[X] The reading group likes to read about wild animals.

[O] This week, they will read about beavers, foxes, and zebras.

146   Daily Fundamentals • EMC 3241 • © Evan-Moor Corp.

Page 147

Name _____

Day 2 | Week 28

Language

Read the sentence. Write the correct word to finish the sentence.

1. I will be __there__ soon.
   their   there

2. Is that __their__ house?
   their   there

3. I've been __there__ before.
   their   there

Math

Circle the two shapes that can be used to make the bigger shape.

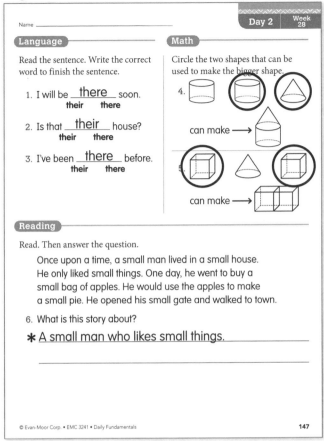

can make →

can make →

Reading

Read. Then answer the question.

Once upon a time, a small man lived in a small house. He only liked small things. One day, he went to buy a small bag of apples. He would use the apples to make a small pie. He opened his small gate and walked to town.

6. What is this story about?

* A small man who likes small things.

© Evan-Moor Corp. • EMC 3241 • Daily Fundamentals   147

Page 148

Name _____

Day 3 | Week 28

Language

Read the sentence. Write the correct word to finish the sentence.

1. Do you __know__ him?
   no   know

2. There is __no__ more milk.
   no   know

3. I __know__ you are right.
   no   know

Math

Draw a new shape using the two shapes given.

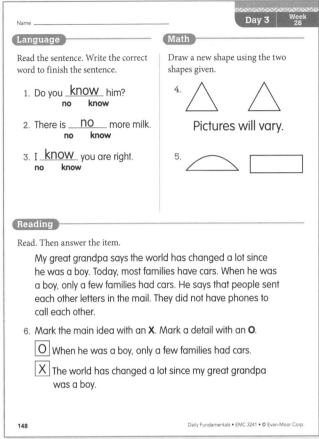

4.

Pictures will vary.

5.

Reading

Read. Then answer the item.

My great grandpa says the world has changed a lot since he was a boy. Today, most families have cars. When he was a boy, only a few families had cars. He says that people sent each other letters in the mail. They did not have phones to call each other.

6. Mark the main idea with an **X**. Mark a detail with an **O**.

[O] When he was a boy, only a few families had cars.

[X] The world has changed a lot since my great grandpa was a boy.

148   Daily Fundamentals • EMC 3241 • © Evan-Moor Corp.

Page 149

Name _____

Day 4 | Week 28

Language

Read the sentence. Write the correct word to finish the sentence.

1. That is __our__ cat's bowl.
   our   hour

2. We start school in one __hour__.
   our   hour

3. Let's have milk with __our__ cookies.
   our   hour

Math

Draw a line from the group of shapes to the new shape you can make.

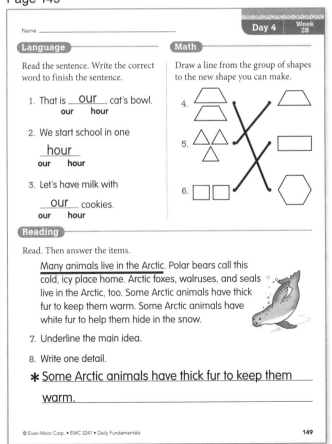

4.

5.

6.

Reading

Read. Then answer the items.

Many animals live in the Arctic. Polar bears call this cold, icy place home. Arctic foxes, walruses, and seals live in the Arctic, too. Some Arctic animals have thick fur to keep them warm. Some Arctic animals have white fur to help them hide in the snow.

7. Underline the main idea.

8. Write one detail.

* Some Arctic animals have thick fur to keep them warm.

© Evan-Moor Corp. • EMC 3241 • Daily Fundamentals   149

Page 150

Name _____

Day 5 | Week 28

Language

Read the sentence. Write the correct word to finish the sentence.

1. The bees are in __their__ hive.
   their   there

2. The bear went __to__ its cave.
   to   two

3. The forest is near __our__ house.
   our   hour

Math

Draw a line from the group of shapes to the new shape you can make.

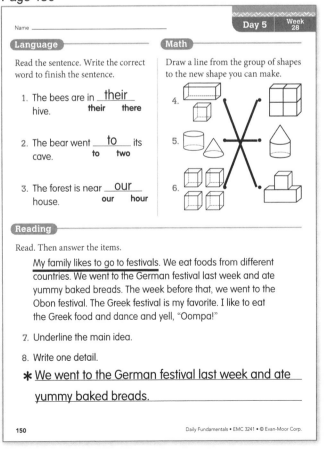

4.

5.

6.

Reading

Read. Then answer the items.

My family likes to go to festivals. We eat foods from different countries. We went to the German festival last week and ate yummy baked breads. The week before that, we went to the Obon festival. The Greek festival is my favorite. I like to eat the Greek food and dance and yell, "Oompa!"

7. Underline the main idea.

8. Write one detail.

* We went to the German festival last week and ate yummy baked breads.

150   Daily Fundamentals • EMC 3241 • © Evan-Moor Corp.

Page 151

Name _____

Day 1 | Week 29

Language

Read the sentence. Write the meaning of the bold word.

1. Grandma used a brush to **scrub** the dirty carpet.

   Scrub means ___to clean___
   to buy   to clean

Math

Look at the shape. Mark **equal** or **unequal** to tell about the shape's parts.

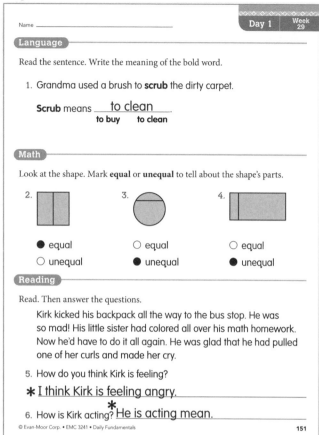

2. ● equal
   ○ unequal

3. ○ equal
   ● unequal

4. ○ equal
   ● unequal

Reading

Read. Then answer the questions.

Kirk kicked his backpack all the way to the bus stop. He was so mad! His little sister had colored all over his math homework. Now he'd have to do it all again. He was glad that he had pulled one of her curls and made her cry.

5. How do you think Kirk is feeling?

✳ I think Kirk is feeling angry.

6. How is Kirk acting? He is acting mean.

© Evan-Moor Corp. • EMC 3241 • Daily Fundamentals   151

Page 152

Name _____

Day 2 | Week 29

Language

Read the sentence. Write the meaning of the bold word.

1. The sleepy parents **awoke** when the baby cried.

   Awoke means ___woke up___
   woke up   ran

Math

Look at the shape. Mark **equal** or **unequal** to tell about the shape's parts.

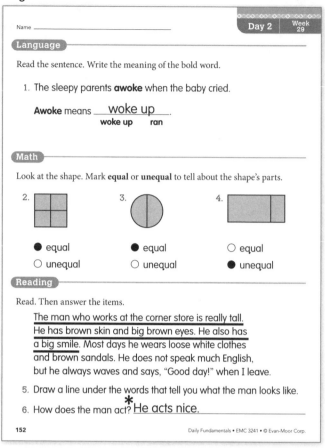

2. ● equal
   ○ unequal

3. ● equal
   ○ unequal

4. ○ equal
   ● unequal

Reading

Read. Then answer the items.

The man who works at the corner store is really tall. He has brown skin and big brown eyes. He also has a big smile. Most days he wears loose white clothes and brown sandals. He does not speak much English, but he always waves and says, "Good day!" when I leave.

5. Draw a line under the words that tell you what the man looks like.

6. How does the man act? ✳ He acts nice.

152   Daily Fundamentals • EMC 3241 • © Evan-Moor Corp.

Page 153

Name _____

Day 3 | Week 29

Language

Read the sentence. Write the meaning of the bold word.

1. Lincoln School puts on a Christmas **play** every year.

   In this sentence, **play** means a story acted out
   to have fun   a story acted out

Math

Circle the shape if it has equal parts.

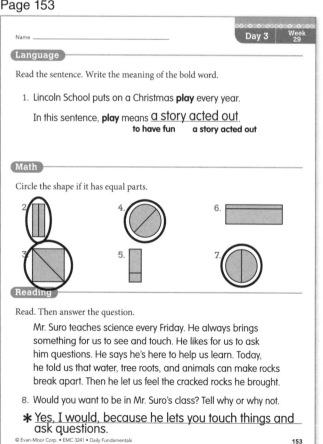

Reading

Read. Then answer the question.

Mr. Suro teaches science every Friday. He always brings something for us to see and touch. He likes for us to ask him questions. He says he's here to help us learn. Today, he told us that water, tree roots, and animals can make rocks break apart. Then he let us feel the cracked rocks he brought.

8. Would you want to be in Mr. Suro's class? Tell why or why not.

✳ Yes, I would, because he lets you touch things and ask questions.

© Evan-Moor Corp. • EMC 3241 • Daily Fundamentals   153

Page 154

Name _____

Day 4 | Week 29

Language

Read the sentence. Write the meaning of the bold word.

1. A black **fly** landed on my dinner plate.

   In this sentence, **fly** means ___an insect___
   an insect   to move through the air

Math

Circle the shape if it has equal parts.

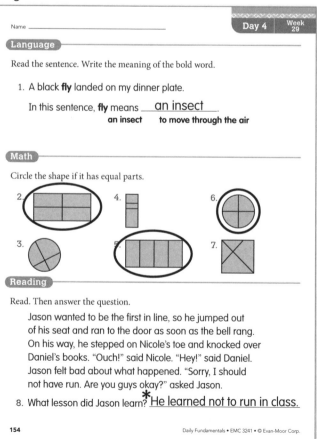

Reading

Read. Then answer the question.

Jason wanted to be the first in line, so he jumped out of his seat and ran to the door as soon as the bell rang. On his way, he stepped on Nicole's toe and knocked over Daniel's books. "Ouch!" said Nicole. "Hey!" said Daniel. Jason felt bad about what happened. "Sorry, I should not have run. Are you guys okay?" asked Jason.

8. What lesson did Jason learn? He learned not to run in class.

154   Daily Fundamentals • EMC 3241 • © Evan-Moor Corp.

These answers will vary. Examples are given.

Page 155

Day 5 | Week 29

Language

Read the sentence. Write the meaning of the bold word.

1. The baseball player has a strong **bat**.

   In this sentence, **bat** means <u>an object used to</u> hit

   an animal   **an object used to hit**

Math

Draw a line on the shape to give it two equal parts.

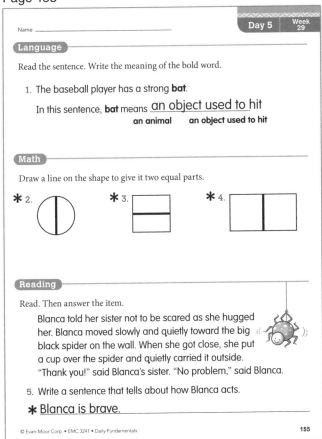

✳ 2.   ✳ 3.   ✳ 4.

Reading

Read. Then answer the item.

Blanca told her sister not to be scared as she hugged her. Blanca moved slowly and quietly toward the big black spider on the wall. When she got close, she put a cup over the spider and quietly carried it outside. "Thank you!" said Blanca's sister. "No problem," said Blanca.

5. Write a sentence that tells about how Blanca acts.

✳ <u>Blanca is brave.</u>

Page 156

Day 1 | Week 30

Language

Read the paragraph. Think about what the bold word means.

The cafeteria is **huge**! All 500 students can eat lunch in it at the same time.

1. Write a sentence about a place you've been that is **huge**.

   <u>Sentences will vary.</u>

Math

Mark **halves** or **fourths** to tell about the shape's parts.

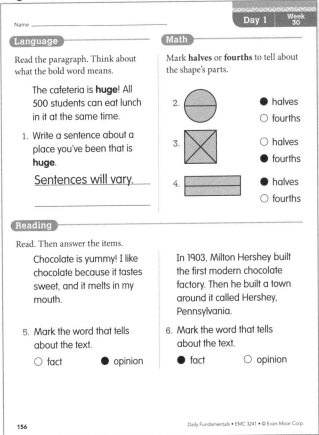

2. ● halves   ○ fourths

3. ○ halves   ● fourths

4. ● halves   ○ fourths

Reading

Read. Then answer the items.

Chocolate is yummy! I like chocolate because it tastes sweet, and it melts in my mouth.

In 1903, Milton Hershey built the first modern chocolate factory. Then he built a town around it called Hershey, Pennsylvania.

5. Mark the word that tells about the text.

   ○ fact   ● opinion

6. Mark the word that tells about the text.

   ● fact   ○ opinion

Page 157

Day 2 | Week 30

Language

Read the paragraph. Think about what the bold word means.

My sister is **kind**. She helps me with my chores. She lets me share her snack and play with her toys.

1. Write a sentence about a person who is **kind**.

   <u>Sentences will vary.</u>

Math

Circle the shape in the pair that shows halves.

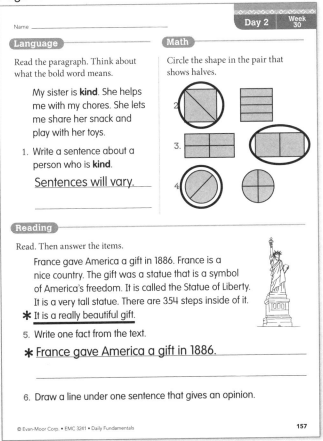

2.
3.
4.

Reading

Read. Then answer the items.

France gave America a gift in 1886. France is a nice country. The gift was a statue that is a symbol of America's freedom. It is called the Statue of Liberty. It is a very tall statue. There are 354 steps inside of it.
✳ <u>It is a really beautiful gift.</u>

5. Write one fact from the text.

✳ <u>France gave America a gift in 1886.</u>

6. Draw a line under one sentence that gives an opinion.

Page 158

Day 3 | Week 30

Language

Read the paragraph. Think about what the bold word means.

The school bus is **crowded**. Kids fill every seat. They can hardly fit their backpacks.

1. Write a sentence about a place you've been that is **crowded**.

   <u>Sentences will vary.</u>

Math

Circle the shape in the pair that shows fourths.

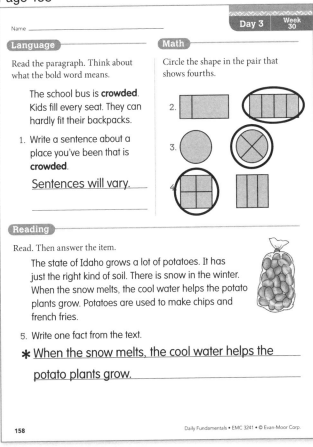

2.
3.
4.

Reading

Read. Then answer the item.

The state of Idaho grows a lot of potatoes. It has just the right kind of soil. There is snow in the winter. When the snow melts, the cool water helps the potato plants grow. Potatoes are used to make chips and french fries.

5. Write one fact from the text.

✳ <u>When the snow melts, the cool water helps the potato plants grow.</u>

Page 159

Name _____

Day 4 | Week 30

Language

Read the paragraph. Think about what the bold word means.

"Don't cut your hand," warned Grandma. "The roses are pretty, but the thorns are **sharp**!" she said.

1. Write a sentence about something **sharp**.

Sentences will vary.

_____

Math

Write **whole**, **half**, or **fourth** to tell about the shaded part of the shape.

2. 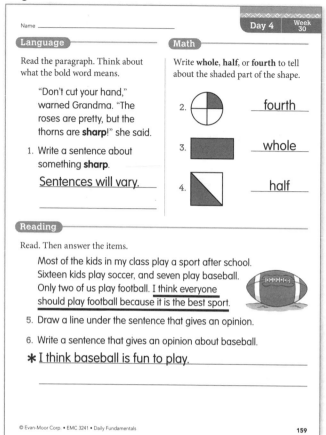 fourth

3. whole

4. half

Reading

Read. Then answer the items.

Most of the kids in my class play a sport after school. Sixteen kids play soccer, and seven play baseball. Only two of us play football. <u>I think everyone should play football because it is the best sport.</u>

5. Draw a line under the sentence that gives an opinion.

6. Write a sentence that gives an opinion about baseball.

✱ <u>I think baseball is fun to play.</u>

_____

Page 160

Name _____

Day 5 | Week 30

Language

Read the paragraph. Think about what the bold word means.

Our new puppy is really **shy**. It hides under the chair and watches Mom and Dad. It will only come out to see me.

1. Write a sentence about someone who is **shy**.

<u>Sentences will vary.</u>

Math

Draw a line or lines on the shape to show halves or fourths.

2. Give the shape halves.

✱ [rectangle with vertical line]

3. Give the shape fourths.

[circle with lines]

Reading

Read. Then answer the items.

Theodor Seuss Geisel was born in 1904. He loved to draw, and he loved to go to the zoo. Theodor became "Dr. Seuss" when he started writing books for children. He wrote *The Cat in the Hat*. He also wrote *Green Eggs and Ham*.

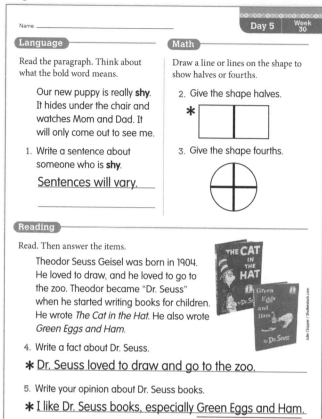

4. Write a fact about Dr. Seuss.

✱ <u>Dr. Seuss loved to draw and go to the zoo.</u>

5. Write your opinion about Dr. Seuss books.

✱ <u>I like Dr. Seuss books, especially Green Eggs and Ham.</u>

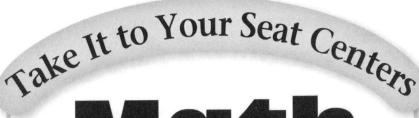

Take It to Your Seat Centers

Math

Take It to Your Seat Centers

Grades K-6

Independent practice, perfect for students at all levels.

Take It to Your Seat Centers: Math

Hands-on practice of core math skills! Each of the 12 centers focuses on key math concepts and presents skill practice in engaging visual and tactile activities. The easy-to-assemble centers include full-color cards and mats, directions, answer keys, and student record forms. Ideal for any classroom and to support RTI or ELLs. 160 full-color pages. Correlated to state standards and Common Core State Standards.

www.evan-moor.com/tmcent

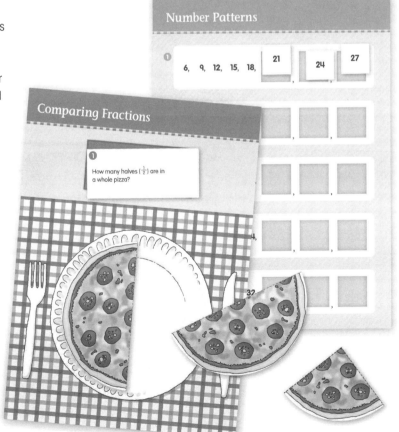

	Teacher's Edition Print		Teacher's Edition E-book
GRADE	**EMC**	**GRADE**	**EMC**
K	3070	K	3070i
1	3071	1	3071i
2	3072	2	3072i
3	3073	3	3073i
4	3074	4	3074i
5	3075	5	3075i
6	3076	6	3076i

Daily Word Problems

Bestseller!

Grades 1–6

Daily Word Problems is the perfect resource to improve students' problem-solving skills. The all-new word problems are written to support current math standards and provide consistent spiral review of math concepts.

- 36 weeks of activities give practice of grade-level math concepts such as addition, multiplication, fractions, logic, algebra, and more.

- Monday through Thursday's activities present a one- or two-step word problem, while Friday's format is more extensive and requires multiple steps.

- The multi-step problems require students to incorporate **higher-order thinking skills.**

128 pages. Correlated to current standards.
www.evan-moor.com/dwp

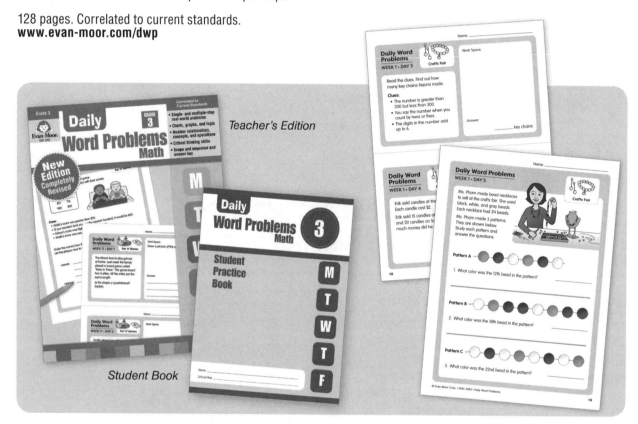

Teacher's Edition

Student Book

Order the format right for you

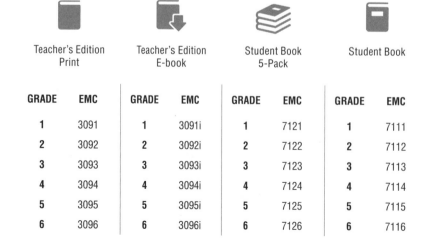

Teacher's Edition Print		Teacher's Edition E-book		Student Book 5-Pack		Student Book	
GRADE	EMC	GRADE	EMC	GRADE	EMC	GRADE	EMC
1	3091	1	3091i	1	7121	1	7111
2	3092	2	3092i	2	7122	2	7112
3	3093	3	3093i	3	7123	3	7113
4	3094	4	3094i	4	7124	4	7114
5	3095	5	3095i	5	7125	5	7115
6	3096	6	3096i	6	7126	6	7116